VERMOUTH

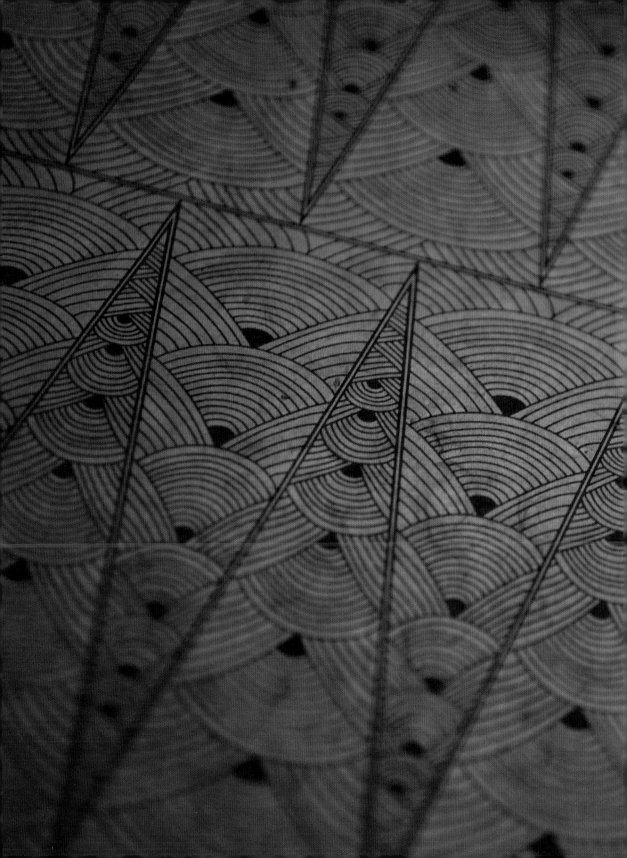

VERMOUTH

A SPIRITED REVIVAL, WITH 40 MODERN COCKTAILS

ADAM FORD

THE COUNTRYMAN PRESS
A division of W. W. Norton & Company
Independent Publishers Since 1923

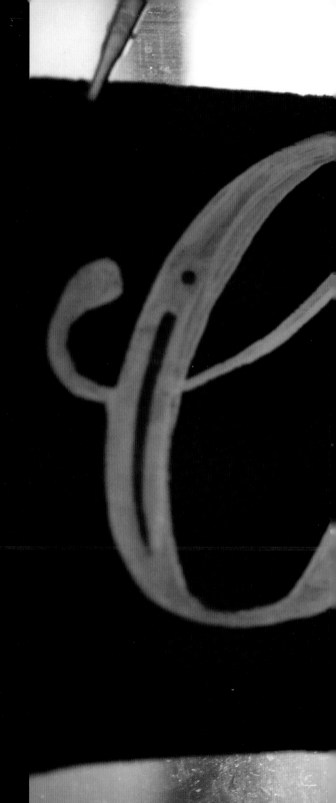

For information about permission to
reproduce selections from this book,
write to Permissions, The Countryman Press,
500 Fifth Avenue, New York, NY 10110

For information about special discounts for
bulk purchases, please contact W. W. Norton
Special Sales at specialsales@wwnorton.com
or 800-233-4830

Interior Design by Nick Caruso
Manufacturing by Toppan Leefung

The Countryman Press
www.countrymanpress.com

A division of W. W. Norton & Company, Inc.
500 Fifth Avenue, New York, NY 10110
www.wwnorton.com

978-1-68268-487-0 (pbk.)

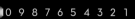

10 9 8 7 6 5 4 3 2 1

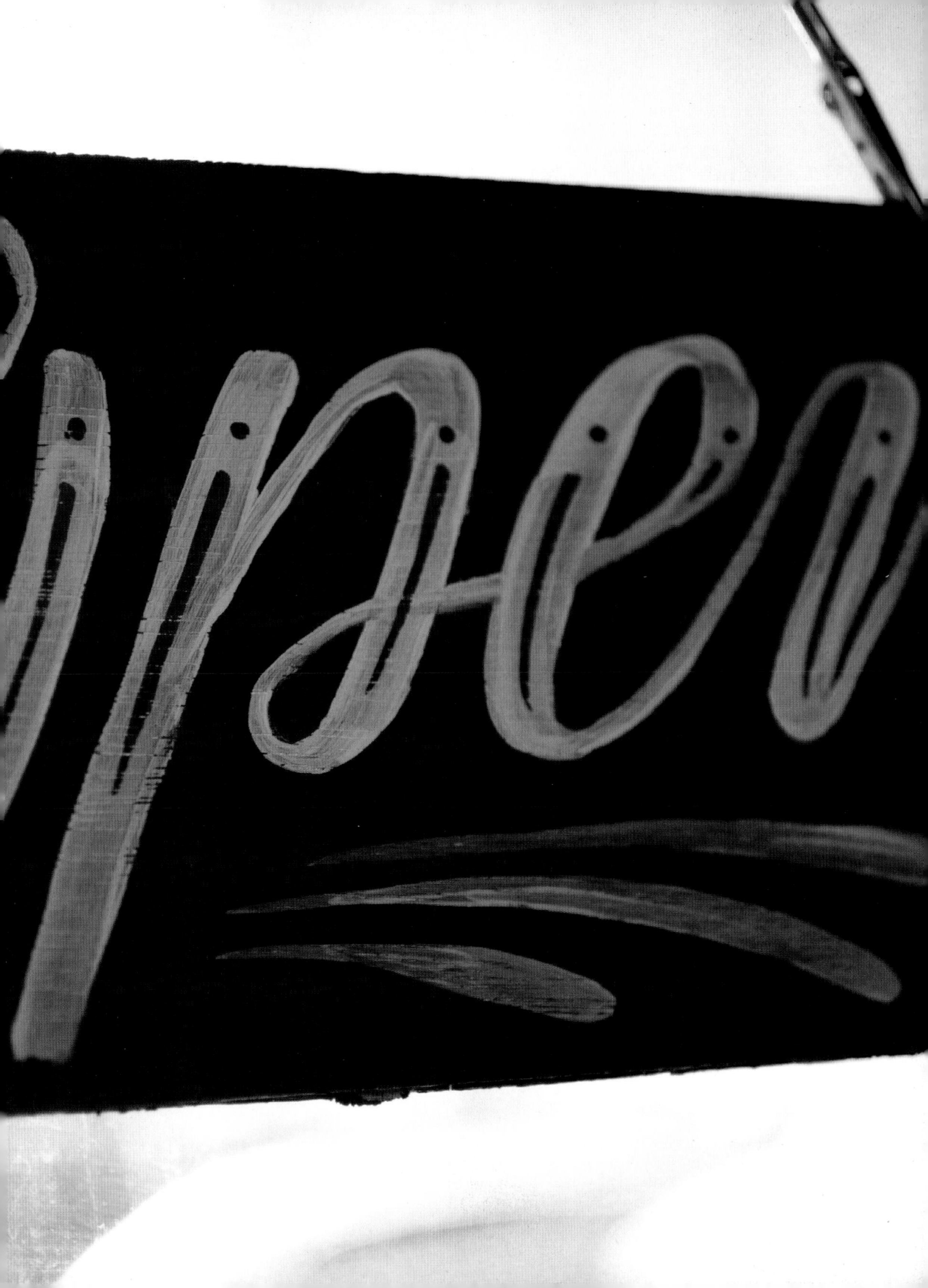

To Glynis, Anker, and Tessa

CONTENTS

INTRODUCTION

"Why did you want to make vermouth?"

The gifted wine and spirits writer Amy Zavatto asked me this question during an interview for an article about my reserve vermouth. It's not the first time I've been asked this, and I love it every time. Now that I've written this book, I expect to be asked the related follow-up: Why would you write a comprehensive book on vermouth? Also a great question, and one that I'd like to answer right from the start.

I wrote this book because I fell deeply in love with a delicious aromatized wine while walking through the Italian Alps. And that led me to create Atsby Vermouth, which was my first attempt to accomplish the Platonic ideal of a perfect vermouth. Then, while creating my two signature expressions—Armadillo Cake and Amberthorn—I engaged in David Wondrich-esque research on vermouth's rich history and realized that the story of vermouth in America had never been told. And the story of vermouth's ancient history as it has been reported for the past several years is filled mostly with factual inaccuracies. Despite vermouth being the height of drinking sophistication for generations, its dizzying fall from grace and its rise from the ashes like that rainbow-plumed phoenix in the past couple of years, no one has set this saga to writing. Given that I did the work and had all this information swirling around my mind, and that in the past two years the category has catapulted from laughing-stock to the center of cool, mature sophistication, it occurred to me that it was high time that someone tell this story. To quote Bob Dylan (who provided much of the soundtrack to my writing sessions), *I guess it must be up to me.*

The backstory of Atsby Vermouth is a simple, non-traditional love story. My wife, Glynis, is second-generation Italian and grew up old-school. On most nights before dinner, as a little girl, she saw her mother and stepfather enjoying sweet Italian vermouth in a nondescript tumbler. On special occasions, such as the Christmas Eve Feast of the Seven Fishes, when the house was filled with friends and family, the fireplace crackled, and garlic, marinara sauce, and fresh fish permeated the air, her mother would give her a small glass of her own (more like a taste). But those sips, as minuscule in volume as they were, burned into her mind an association of vermouth with the feelings of joy, love, and celebration with friends and family.

Glynis and I had our first date at an old speakeasy at 86 Bedford Street in the West Village (the building crumbled a few years later). She ordered a glass of sweet vermouth—chilled, up—displaying rare style and confidence. *Who orders vermouth?* I thought, and was immediately drawn in by the mystery. I asked her about it, and she responded nonchalantly that it was a drink to have with people you feel connected to. She paused, then added, "And I can drink it all night without worrying about how I might behave later." Her tone was sophisticated but not fussy.

I had never tasted vermouth, nor was I interested. I thought I looked cool pouring a dash into a martini glass and then dumping it out. My parents were hippies and didn't drink such old-timey stuff. It had never occurred to me to give it a chance. In the bar that night, I ordered a bottled beer. (The place was historic, surreal, idyllic, but let's face it, the taps hadn't been cleaned since Prohibition.) But I quickly questioned my choice because she came off as so much cooler and more confident than I did.

That first date evolved into moving in together, marriage, and then the financial devastation that would lead to the Lehman Brothers bankruptcy of September 15, 2008, during the aftershocks of which we decided to get away from Manhattan for a while. We set out to hike the Tour du Mont Blanc, which circles the largest mountain in Europe through France, Switzerland, and Italy. We bought a plane ticket online, took off of work with only two days' notice, and were in Geneva the next morning. We took a fast, clean train to Chamonix, and,

wearing far-too-heavy backpacks, we bought a map at an outdoors store and a pound of Morbier (really stinky) cheese and a baguette at a corner shop, and walked out of town and toward fields of high grass and mountain wildflowers, opting to bypass the gondola that takes walkers to the top of the first big climb.

We spent a few days hiking over glaciers and snowfields. In mountain huts we slept next to strangers whose language we did not speak, and whose odors were different than ours. When we got back down into the Aosta Valley about a week later, in the serene mountain town of Courmayeur, we rewarded ourselves with a fancy hotel room and an expensive dinner at a small side-street café, a little bit off the main town square. During dinner, my wife noticed that others in the restaurant were drinking vermouth, and of course she ordered a glass. We had never seen the brand before. She took it cellar temperature in a classic Italian wine glass, like everyone else, and loved it.

For the first time I tried it too, and found it unlike anything I'd ever drunk before. The flavors were intriguing, enigmatic, and distended. I asked the bartender (in Spanish) what the ingredients were and he told us (in Italian) that—as with all vermouths—it was a highly guarded secret, but that everyone had their opinions as to some of the ingredients. An Israeli couple next to us overheard and suggested a few possibilities: Maybe gentian? Or angelica? Certainly some cinnamon. The night ended with a list of almost a dozen potential candidates that I wrote down on the back of a napkin, sadly long since lost.

We closed out the restaurant, and despite the amount we had drunk, we walked back to our hotel room still sober and excited, holding hands like a couple of junior-high kids. While I looked at her and she looked toward the stars, I asked Glynis what she wanted to do when we got back to America. She said she wanted more nights like the one we had just had. More joy talking to strangers and learning new things. More feelings of connectedness and passion and excitement about things to come. Carrying the warmth from that evening, we finished hiking around Mont Blanc and made it back to Rougemont, Switzerland, where an art collector friend warmly welcomed us. He took us out for Raclette to fill us up and replace some weight we had lost.

When we returned home, for many nights we cooked the simple meals we had eaten along the walk through Italy: sautéed wild mushrooms over polenta, sliced flank steak over a bed of arugula, and Parmesan sprinkled with freshly-squeezed lemon juice. Each meal started with a glass of vermouth. What we were able to purchase back in America, however, was nothing like what we had experienced in Courmayeur. I thought the vermouths we purchased and were drinking were mediocre, at best. They paled in comparison. They were like buying a suit off the rack after years of having tailor-made; it was fine, but you didn't feel like you were at the top of the food chain. One night, perhaps searching for that ineffable feeling, Glynis made the offhand comment of how wonderful it would be to be back in Italy drinking that vermouth on that side street off the town square. That vermouth, we both knew, even if we never said it, had so much more flavor, so much more intensity; it filled our mouths with joy and secrecy. She asked why we couldn't bottle that feeling. Then it struck us. We could create a new vermouth, an Americana-styled one that both improved upon the European brands found in America and reminded us of that perfect evening in that sublime mountain town.

I love attempting the impossible. I spent countless hours at the New York Public Library uncovering long forgotten and split-spine books on vermouth's history, and I started buying and tasting every botanical I could find. The Internet, for all of its wonders, turned out to be useless in this arena. There was practically nothing written on vermouth at all. With my lawyerly indefatigable grit, though, I eventually learned that vermouth used to be a wildly fashionable drink in America, and that there were once a couple hundred American wineries producing it, the majority of which were in New York. I learned that my Italian-American grandparents drank it, albeit in small doses on special occasions. Of course studying history wasn't the answer; I needed to actually begin testing out different ratios, different forms of the botanicals, fresh, dried, crushed, and different maceration periods.

After painstaking research, figuring out entirely different botanical than the ones supposedly used by the European brands, trying out new blends and ideas, and fantastic failures, I created the formula for a new vermouth, loosely based on historical recipes but updated with contemporary knowledge of botany, wine, and spirit creation. The formula was tested by a sommelier who proclaimed that it perfectly hit all five tastes—sweet, sour, salty, bitter, and umami—and it was declared ready to bring vermouth into the twenty-first century. The ineffable quality turned out to be simply using the highest quality, locally sourced base ingredients and caring a great deal for the process.

And boy, have times changed since then! Atsby Vermouth was the first commercially produced vermouth in the Northeast and quickly became one of the largest American craft vermouth producers, spreading out from New York City like wildfire. Within its first year, distributors around the country and in Europe picked up Atsby. It has become the most critically acclaimed vermouth produced in America. *Wine Spectator* declared that we gave vermouth its reputation back. Other American producers followed (there are now at least a dozen American craft vermouth producers), with dozens more in the works and foreign brands from all over the world now being imported into the United States.

Meanwhile, in Europe, vermouth has taken over as *the* drink. In Spain, they call it simply, *to do vermouth*—by which they mean the ritual of drinking vermouth and enjoying a light snack before dinner and a night out. From Australia to England, new craft producers are releasing novel and innovative takes on the product across the globe. In America, too, finally, amazingly, we're starting to enjoy vermouth on its own. In New York, where vermouth was actually born in America, Michelin-rated restaurants are serving vermouth straight, even by the bottle on wine lists, and major spirits publications are tripping over themselves to tout vermouth as *the* trend of the moment. In other words, it seemed like the perfect time to write this all down.

Salute! I hope you enjoy it.

AUTHOR'S NOTE

Anyone who has been paying attention to the recent resurgence in vermouth knows about the debate over whether American vermouth producers—who have been largely, if not entirely, responsible for this newfound excitement—can really call their product "vermouth." American producers (with extremely limited exceptions) do not use wormwood as an ingredient, and as the proponents of the anti-American vermouth position will tell you, vermouth without wormwood is not truly vermouth.

As the rest of this book will make clear, I do not think this is a real debate. Yet I feel compelled to lend my voice to the discussion. The large multi-national spirits brands have spent vast sums of money these past three years spreading their view of how to define vermouth—a view that by all accounts is only a few years old and contrary to the historical record. This view is not supported by history, facts, or common sense, yet because the big companies have had the money to spread it, it has become the prevailing view.

In a large way, I've always thought of the debate about wormwood in vermouth as an exercise in futility. If wormwood was essential for vermouth, well then, wormwood would be essential to vermouth and no one would be talking about it. It would just be obvious. American producers would have released their "vermouths" and people would have taken a sip, rolled their eyes, and proclaimed, "This is not vermouth." Obviously that hasn't happened.

Still, I have attempted to present both sides of the argument fairly and accurately so that you can weigh both and come to a reasoned position. Interspersed throughout this book are thirty-seven recipes of the best vermouth cocktails in the world. Regardless of which side of the divide you fall on, I trust we can all agree that the cocktails in here, if drunk at the right times and in moderation, will make your life richer and fuller.

chapter one

THE HISTORY OF VERMOUTH

Vermouth is an aromatized wine that possesses an indescribable and complex flavor profile. It can be made with various botanicals historically believed to have positive health benefits, but first and foremost it is formulated to be drunk for pleasure. The origin of its name is, amazingly, unknown. For over two centuries people have hypothesized that its name comes from the German word for wormwood (German: *Wermut*, Latin: *Artemisia absinthium*), but, as I will discuss later, its connection to this one particular plant and a mythical German beverage bearing a similar name is tenuous given the historical record.

   This chapter is intended to be the first attempt to discuss this product's actual history, or at least a small slice of it. There has never been a comprehensive review of vermouth's history, and the written record is woefully incomplete and filled with repeated inaccuracies. I do not profess to have figured it all out. The chronology stretches at least 10,000 years and includes humans from every major geographical area (with the exception of North America!), and therefore anything I could attempt here will be obviously, woefully incomplete. Given that, the best I can do is offer a conceptual history and touch upon some of its high points: where we know it started, how it has evolved, and where it is now.

As it turns out, vermouth, or at least its original prototype of a wine infused with botanicals, happens to be the world's oldest alcoholic beverage.[1] It beats unadulterated wine, vodka, and single malt scotch by a mile. For as long as human beings have been imbibing alcohol, they have been infusing their fermented beverages with various herbs, spices, barks, roots, petals, and other edible plant parts for two primary purposes: first, to improve the flavor of the base alcohol, and second, to take advantage of the botanicals' medicinal properties.* Indeed, for much of the history of human alcohol consumption, there has been a blurry line—if one existed at all—between drinking for pleasure and drinking for health. Early humans believed, rightfully so, that aromatics possessed various health benefits. While many of these claims have been discovered to be overblown or inaccurate, many were surprisingly on-point.

CHINA

This story starts in an unlikely place: Jiahu, in the Henan Province of north-central China where the Huai River merges with the Yellow River, the site of an original burial ground that housed dozens of pottery and a salmagundi of artifacts from the Neolithic period, ca. 6200–5600. Thankfully for us, world-renowned alcoholic-beverage historian Patrick McGovern and his team traveled to Jiahu and chemically analyzed sixteen shards from a range of jars and jugs that appeared to have contained liquids. Five analytical methods[2] were used to identify the chemical constituents of the pottery and liquid extracts.[3] The analysis revealed the presence of tartaric acid, which meant that the beverage was a mixture of wine, made from either grapes or hawthorn fruit, with honey mead and

---

* This is not to say that the base flavor was bad, or that the wine was spoiled, as is commonly suggested. It is clear that humans have been meticulous in their production of aromatized wine for 10,000 years, and there is little evidence to suggest that the addition of herbs and spices was merely a way to mask bad flavor; the intent was rather to add additional flavor as well as to take advantage of the plants' medicinal properties, including its aid in digestion.

rice malt. While this drink's flavor profile may appear a peculiar mish-mash of unmixables at first pass, this combination gives us clues as to what this first vermouth would have tasted like. The hawthorn berry tastes something like a cross between a cranberry and a strawberry, with a sweet first flavor and tart aftertaste. The honey would have added both sweetness and the floral notes of local wildflowers. The unhulled rice malt, fermented on sake yeast, would have added the bitter, sour profiles, balancing the sweetness of the honey and the tartness of the fruit. The drink would have been highly aromatic; modern incarnations of it have been found "exotic [and] immensely satisfying" and come surprisingly close to hitting all known taste profiles, as modern vermouths attempt to do.

It is hypothesized that this beverage would have been drunk during special occasions, particularly in connection with rituals for when a community member died. A highly formalized ceremony involving dancing, music, and feasting would be capped off when a descendant of the deceased drank for himself and the ancestors.

Shortly after the discovery, McGovern was offered the opportunity to analyze the liquid contents of an ornate bronze vessel found in the extensively excavated ancient city of Yinxu, located about 300 kilometers north of Jiahu. Yinxu was a bustling metropolis about 3,000 years ago, and contained various examples of ceremonial vessels used for serving wine to the upper class ca. 1250–1000 BCE. Despite being 3,000 years old, the liquid inside the vessel was still highly fragrant, "slightly oxidized like sherry, with a perfumed bouquet."[4] Interestingly, this beverage was quite different than the one found at Jiahu. McGovern found no honey and no fruit, but instead a very special millet wine that had been aromatized with either chrysanthemum flower or resin from the elemi family of fragrant trees. Even by this time in ancient China, chrysanthemum wine had a long and storied history, having a unique flavor and properties to color the wine yellow (which symbolized the emperor). Like the hawthorn berries, which are now known to have various medicinal uses as a diuretic, astringent, and as a cardiac tonic for heart troubles, the triterpenoids compounds found in elemi and chrysanthemum have antioxidant properties, meaning that Chinese beverage makers may have been aware of the medicinal qualities of these flowers and leaves by this time, and intentionally making "medicinal" wines.

McGovern also tested samples from another upper-class tomb from the late Shang Dynasty that was found about 250 kilometers east of Zhengzhou in Changzikou. The site held almost a hundred bronze vessels, half of which still contained liquid. These vessels however did not contain millet wine or the grog found in Jihau but rather a highly specialized rice wine that had been aromatized with several botanicals. This sample also maintained its balm for 3,000 years, although the camphor smell was less intense. The chemical analysis and historical research led McGovern to conclude that this rice wine had probably been aromatized with tree resin from China fir and with a flower, which was probably chrysanthemum or an herb in the *Artemisia* family, likely *Artemisia argyi*, otherwise known as Chinese mugwort. This finding suggests that there was a systematic improvement and refinement of an herbal wine industry over several millennia and that the herbal infusions became more complex and—we can only imagine—delicious. Indeed, excavations in the Shang dynasty city of Taixi uncovered a wine infused with peach, plum, Chinese jujube pits, in addition to the seeds of sweet clover, jasmine, and hemp.[5]

Significantly, these herbal wines were found in upper-class tombs, and according to inscriptions in Shang oracle bones, the Shang palace administration included officials who made the beverages, which sometimes were inspected by the king. According to McGovern, these fermented beverages and other foods were offered as sacrifices to royal ancestors in various bronze vessels, likely accompanied by elite feasting. Even more significant is that these were clearly "medicinal wines" with anesthetic and antimicrobial properties. Thus, the historical evidence suggests that humans have been infusing botanicals into their wines for health reasons for at least several thousand years.

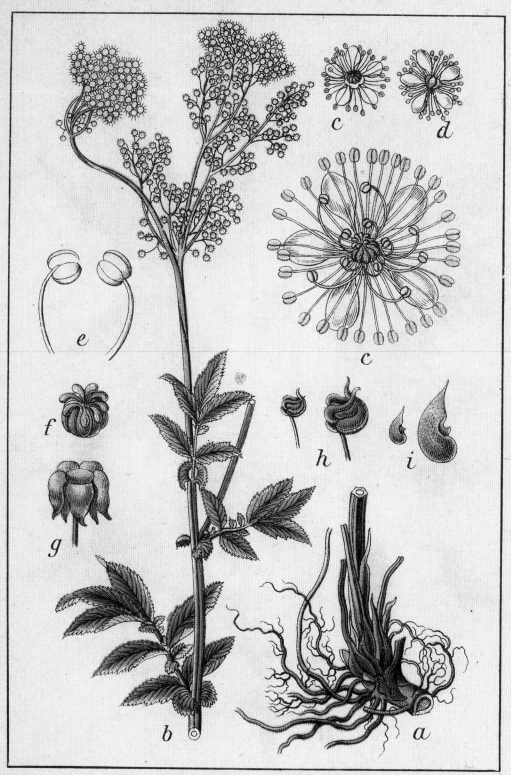

Meadowsweet

THE MIDDLE EAST

It wasn't just the Chinese who learned to infuse their wine with botanicals. If they were in fact the first, the rest of the world wasn't far behind, particularly the Middle East. Chemical analysis of pottery shards dating back to ca. 5400–5000 BCE, found in what was once the kitchen of a home in a small Neolithic village called Hajji Firuz Tepe in the northern Zagros Mountains of modern-day Iran, revealed wines infused with terebinth tree resin, (the terebinth tree, a member of the pistachio family, was widespread throughout the Middle East during this time). Resinated wines (i.e., wines infused with tree resins) have been around for as long as wine has been made and were highly valued throughout ancient times. What was most significant about this finding was that the jars were found in the kitchen of a home, not in a grand tomb, suggesting that by this time various community members may have consumed the drinks, irrespective of social or political class. This isn't to say that beverages mixed for the king and the ruling classes weren't of a higher quality. Certainly the intricately designed serving vessels from the Anatolian highlands (present-day Turkey) from mid- to late second millennium BCE and ancient Hittite texts support the theory that the rulers enjoyed a particularly splendid wine, likely an herbal blend that included honey or grape must, tree oil (olive oil?), and sea water, as well as a fruit puree.[6]

Significantly, there is no archaeological evidence of direct contact between China and the Middle East during the Neolithic Period, so it appears that these peoples had begun aromatizing their wines quite independently of each other. Other writers have suggested that the history of vermouth was linear, starting in China and systematically making its way across the world, but there is no evidence of this single source distribution. It is not until the first millennium BCE that there is proof of direct contact and cross-fertilization of ideas and technology through cross-continental trade routes. Once this confluence of cultures occurs, the move toward more specialized and sophisticated herb-flavored wines takes off.

ANCIENT EGYPT

The Ancient Egyptians, too, knew how to throw together a batch of herbal wine, and their drinks approached a taste and sophistication that very well could find success on the shelves of a premier wine shop in New York City today. Pedanius Dioscorides, the first century Roman physician of Greek origin, wrote that the Egyptians worshipped their sun god Ra with a highly fragrant drink made of juniper, the exotic myrrh, and several aromatic herbs mixed with honey and wine.[7] Once again it was Patrick McGovern who had the honor of analyzing the archaeological samples, specifically an early sample from a multi-chambered tomb at Abydos on the middle Nile River in Upper Egypt, which has been dated by radiocarbon determinations to ca. 3150 BCE. The tomb was built in the desert and belongs to one of the first rulers of the country, Scorpion I, at the beginning of Egyptian dynastic history.

This sample from the tomb of Scorpion I contained eight terpenoid compounds, which results in an unclear historical record of which herbs were infused in this wine. There are two competing theories: one states that the wine was infused with as few as three herbs: savory, *Artemisia sieberi* (a member of the wormwood family), and blue tansy. But because the chemicals found in these herbs occur in seven other herbal genera, others have hypothesized that Egyptian aromatized wine was made by infusing balm, cassia, coriander, germander, mint, sage, and thyme. If this is the case, the Egyptians were making an infused wine in 3150 BCE with as many different flavor components as Imbue Vermouth from Oregon was in 2012.

Putting aside what the chemical analyses show, many of the plants that could account for the compounds found in these ancient wines were not native to Egypt and there is no historical record of them having reached Egypt by this time. Significantly, only cassia and two unidentified plants from the *Satureja* and *Salvia genuses* are possibly native to Egypt. *Artemisia sieberi* is from Iran, and the blue tansy is believed to be native to Morocco—there is no evidence of it being in Egypt at that time. Therefore, it appears historically inaccurate to suggest that any *Artemisia* was in Egyptian aromatized wine as of 3150 BCE.[8]

The Egyptians, like the Chinese before them and the Romans after them, infused their wines with herbs believed to have healing properties. Among the most probable herbal additives to this sample of aromatized wine is coriander, whose importance in ancient Egyptian culture and medicine cannot be understated. (King Tut was buried with half a liter of coriander mericarps.) Coriander is listed in several medical prescriptions from this time. Stomach problems called for drinking a beer mixed with coriander, bryony, flax, and dates. For the treatment of blood in the stool, coriander was to be grated and mixed with chaste tree and another unidentified fruit, infused into beer, strained, and drunk. For treating herpes, an external salve was prepared from coriander seeds, myrrh, and fermented honey. (Don't try this at home; stick with Valtrex.)

The Egyptians continued to improve upon their aromatized wine manufacturing, and by the late first millennium BCE these drinks were being prepared by master artisans who would grind and sieve equal amounts of sweet flag, aromatic rush, terebinth resin, cassia, mint, and possibly *Aspalathus*. This mixture was blended with wine and juniper berries, *Cyperus* and other plants, raisins, frankincense, and then sweetened with honey. The addition of finely ground myrrh completed the recipe.

Significantly, from about the same time as the Abydos wine, native rosemary and mint together with thyme were being added to a fermented emmer wheat or barley beverage at Genó in Spain. Early medieval European beer was also flavored using wild rosemary, bog myrtle, and yarrow.

PERSIA

Iran, not exactly the best country nowadays for a wild night out of cocktails and over-indulgent drinking, holds the distinction of being the birthplace of unadulterated wine, which was first produced around 2500 BCE. Just northeast of the Dasht-e Kavir desert, an Early Bronze Age settlement sprouted that housed an extravagant building that held a few large plaster-coated bowls that at the time contained an herbal wine infused with poppy, ephedra, and marijuana, as well as hemp flowers and seeds, ephedra stem fragments, and various other plants (including *Artemisia*). This drink was called Haoma. The settlement was a stopping point along the Silk Routes, giving it access to new exotic spices.

The potency of this mixed drink is rather fun to imagine. Ephedra stimulates the sympathetic nervous system and causes a slight ecstasy. The tetrahydrocannabinol (THC) in marijuana is also a euphoric and invigorates the imagination (such as imagining where the Funyuns are), and the poppy (i.e., opium) would greatly contribute to hallucinatory experiences. That all of these narcotics were then infused into a wine, which itself obviously affects the human nervous system, reminds me of a night I once had at college. But I digress. This drink (Haoma, not the one from the house party) was often part of a prayer ritual and would result in euphoria as well as "a sharpening of internal and external sensations," where noises found an "extraordinary internal echo, and the conception of time and space is changed." In this state, and while repeating prayers and incantations, drinkers would reach "special realms of consciousness where they witnessed vivid visions."[9] In addition to archeological findings, ancient sacred texts also shed light on this. The beverage also contained auxiliary ingredients, such as "milk, the fat of a bull, and barley grains" all of which had symbolic and ritualistic significance. The beverage was known as a "pain-killer, and its attributes were described as "healing" or "treatment that heals."[10]

All of these findings shouldn't suggest that we actually know very much about the use and creation of herbal wines in ancient history. There are very wide gaps in human knowledge and understanding about this time period, and many of the findings are still open to debate and discussion. (Some still argue that Haoma was made from the urine of a white bull calf or the fly of an agaric mushroom or a fungus that grows on rye and is related to LSD.) And it's still unclear whether these beverages were created and made based solely on local knowledge, or whether travelers traversing the Silk Routes provided additional information about ingredients. Given the lapse of time and the lack of an accurate historical record, it is unlikely that the debates raging around what exactly was included in these various infusions will ever be firmly and conclusively resolved. I would propose, however, that while this information would be interesting, it is not essential to understanding the history of vermouth, any more than understanding what existed before the Big Bang would assist us in understanding our present universe. In other words, vermouth as we understand it has historical roots in the ancient past, but its direct lineage actually only dates from the Renaissance.

THE SILK ROUTES

I have spoken at numerous spirits and cocktail conferences and taught hundreds of classes on the history of vermouth, and usually my opening line is that the story of vermouth is the story of the silk routes. The Silk Routes (or the Silk Road) were a chain of pathways connecting the East (China, India, Persia, Arabia) with the West (the Mediterranean, Roman Empire, Armenia) that linked various traders, merchants, pilgrims, monks, and adventurers.

The most famous of these explorers I think of every time my wife, two kids, and I are in a pool, eyes closed, giggling while one of us is screaming "Marco" and everyone else is splashing away saying "Polo." Incomplete routes allowed some trade as early as 1070 BCE. The Route was mostly complete by the time of Herodotus, the father of modern history, around 475 BCE; the sweet spot of trading began around 206 BCE and exploded with the Roman conquest of Egypt in 30 BCE, by which time the Greco-Roman trade with India had started and citizens of the Roman Empire had gained access to new luxury items, of which new spices were among the most valuable and sought after. Indeed, spices, perfumes, and silk were among the newest, most luxurious and valuable items for its wealthy citizens.

While there are clearly early prototypes of wines infused with herbs and herbal flavors dating back to the Neolithic period (and likely earlier), it is only after trade routes are established, along with the exchange of knowledge and various herbs and spices, that we start getting closer to "modern day vermouth," which is typically an amalgamation of flavors resulting from highly valuable herbs and spices, sometimes originating from far off and distant lands, being infused together to create an entirely new flavor.

During Ptolemaic times, traders stopped along the southern half of Africa's Red Sea coastline and at ports along the Horn of Africa. In addition to elephants and ivory, this part of Africa provided the Romans with various spices including cinnamon, and with aromatic woods such as myrrh and frankincense, both tree resins and the mostly highly demanded aromatics in the ancient world.[11] Frankincense and myrrh from southern Arabia were in serious demand throughout the Mediterranean and traveled routes that went northwest toward Egypt and the coastal cities of the Mediterranean. The Romans were particularly fond of and used costus, bdellium, lyceum, and nard as spices and medicines, all of which came from plants grown in the exotic and distant lands in the high mountains of Kashmir and the Himalayas.[12]

Spices are so commonplace today that it is hard to comprehend just how special they were once considered. Etymology helps a little: "spice" derives from the Latin *species,* meaning an item of special value. Even pepper was considered more valuable than gold and silver; the Caesars treated pepper as a currency. A Tamil poet described the Roman traders in a southern Indian port by noting, "they arrive with gold and depart with pepper."[13] Roman author and naturalist Pliny the Elder (23–79 CE) was known to criticize the vast quantities of Roman gold needed to purchase aromatics from India. Even several centuries later, when the British defeated the Spanish Armada in 1588, King Phillip II of Spain ran out of silver and had to use his warehouses of pepper to even up his balance sheet.

But who could blame the Romans for this infatuation? In addition to spices' aromatic, deeply pleasurable scent and taste, and of course their erotic qualities, the stories of how they were cultivated and obtained were part of their allure. For example, cinnamon, according to Herodotus, was "brought to Arabia by large birds, which carry the sticks to their nests, made of mud, on mountain precipices which no man can climb." The only way to collect these sticks was to "cut up the bodies of dead oxen into very large

joints, and leave them on the ground near the nests. They then scatter, and the birds fly down and carry off the meat to their nests, which are too weak to bear the weight and fall to the ground" so that the workers can collect them and bring them to the Mediterranean.[14] Cassia was not much easier to get, and legends told of the "Arabians cover[ing] their bodies and faces, all but their eyes, with ox-hides and other skins before going out to collect [cassia]. It grows in a shallow lake. The lake and all the country road are infested by winged creatures like bats, which screech horribly and are very fierce. They have to be kept from attacking the men's eyes while they are cutting the cassia."

Given these fanciful tales straight out of *1,001 Nights*, is it any wonder that cinnamon was an aroma of divine worship and sexuality? The biblical adulteress in Exodus sprinkles her bed with cinnamon before suggesting she and her paramour "drink deep of love until the morning, and abandon [them]selves to delight."

By the time Pliny penned his *Natural History* in 77 CE, he had pretty much figured out the game, explaining that "these old tales were invented by the Arabians to raise the price of their goods."[15] But even this knowledge couldn't stop the unquenchable human thirst for exotic scents and flavors to be used as perfumes and drinks and bed coverings so that Romans could abandon themselves to delight.

THE MEDITERRANEAN

The ancient Greeks were known to have mingled their wine with boiled seawater before drinking it, which they thought improved its flavor.* While Hippocrates is credited with using various herbs to treat illnesses, and is believed to have created hundreds of aromatized wines, it is unclear whether Hippocrates himself actually drafted any of these recipes. It is more likely that his followers and students deserve the credit. In any event, peppered wine, from the

---

* Two thousand years later, the world's foremost food and drinks expert Harold McGee shocked the world when he suggested that adding water to wine improved its flavor. Turns out, the Greeks were on to something. In fact, they were on to several things.

Hellenistic period (following the conquests of Alexander), was a mixture of "washed, dried finely ground peppercorns, 8 scruples, attic honey, and old white wine"[16]

The Romans improved upon the Greeks by mingling their wines with many more herbs and spices, in addition to salt water. They had dozens if not hundreds of different recipes for drinking during festivals, or even as part of a daily ritual. These wines were also infused increasingly with purported magical spices such as asafetida, tar, bitumen, pitch, myrrh, aloes, gums, pepper, spikenard, poppies, wormwood, cassia, milk, chalk, bitter almonds, and cypress.[17]

As we have seen, the realization that herbs and spices have positive health benefits and can be used as medicine, both when delivered through wine or another fermented beverage (including vinegar and fish sauce) or through food, can be traced back thousands of years, at least to the Ancient Chinese and Egyptians. The Ancient Greeks, however, were the first to outline a system of medicine based on a holistic view of the body, and to attempt to tie sickness and health to the balance or imbalance of bodily fluids, rather than adhering to the previous belief that sickness was a result of punishment by the Gods.

Hippocrates, the father of medicine, is credited with being the first person to separate religion from medicine, and he came up with a (ultimately incorrect) view of how the body worked. In the fourth century BCE, Hippocrates set forth the ancient doctrine of the "Four Humors," which, people at the time believed, enabled doctors to understand the origin of sickness, and therefore propose a cure. Health and illness were caused by either balance or imbalance, based on the four bodily humors: blood, phlegm, yellow bile, and black bile. These were all naturally occurring in the body, but during specific seasons they could get out of balance and cause illness. By way of example, a cold during the winter was blamed on an overabundance of phlegm; summer dysentery was caused by an overabundance of bile.[18] Central to the treatment of unbalanced humors was the use of herbs. Specific herbs were used to treat all ailments from an uncomplicated upper respiratory infection to the Black

These stylized drawings show the Four Humors—blood, phlegm, black bile, and yellow bile—depicted with their corresponding states.

Plague. When a disease was caused by an overabundance of phlegm, which was considered a cold and moist humor, the patient would head to the local apothecary to be treated with hot and dry remedies: hyssop, cumin, licorice, and ginger syrup, dispensed in wine. Chamomile was used to decrease heat, and lower excessive bile. Humoralism retained its popularity for centuries, largely through the influence of the writings of Galen (131–201 CE), and was

PHLEGMATICUS.

Cui fortuna favet prædam petitum habet, Soll eine Handelschafft beglückt von statten gehen,
Mercator improbus Divitias quærit in undis, so muß man mit Verstand und Geld sich wohl versehen;
per mille pericla vitam exponere solet, und gibt Neptunus Glück auf ungestümen Meer,
pectora quid auri sacra fames non cogit. so bringt die Schiffart, feucht den größten Reichthum her.

Ioh. Michael Probst exc. Aug V.   C. P. S. C. M.   I. Mohar Folio N.º 3.

SANGUINEUS.

Omnia vincit amor, et nos cedamus amori, Venus, mit ihrem Kind, kan Helden Herz besiegen,
at foné Cerere, et Baccho friget Venus müssen auch Bacchus offt verliebte Zan betrügen;
sola: hæc nostra mere tuus est Vita: Spiel und Kartenspiel auch leicht beisamen seyn,
Apollo solus liberales fovet artes. Apollo fast allein die freye Künste ein.

Ioh. Michael Probst exc. et del. Aug V.   C. P. S. C. M.   I. Mohar Folio N.º 3.

only decisively displaced in 1858 by Rudolf Virchow's newly published theories of cellular pathology.

Around the time of Hippocrates, and over the next few centuries, the first "medical texts" came into print. Theophrastus published his *Study of Plants* in 310 BCE, and the first manual of Pharmacopeia, *Materia Medica,* was written by Pedanius Dioscorides a few decades after the time of Jesus Christ. Celsus'

On Medicine and Pliny the Elder's *Natural History* were also published in the first century. All of these works discussed—in staggering detail given the time in which they were written—purported therapeutic uses for hundreds of different plants, herbs, and spices. Dioscorides is believed to have traveled with Roman Emperor Nero's army and to have collected herbs and spices, also gathering knowledge on their purported health effects. *De Materia Medica* lists about 1,000 plant based "drugs" and close to 5,000 medicinal uses for these drugs.[19] Dioscorides also lists just under 400 medical properties for these herbs and spices, including antiseptic, laxative, appetite stimulant, antidote against poison, and on and on. Dioscorides' treatment of sugar is representative of the type of medical information included in his opus: "There is also a substance called sakkharon, a sort of crystallized honey, in India and Arabia. It is not unlike salt in its texture, and can be crunched between the teeth like salt. It is laxative, good to drink dissolved in water, and beneficial in bladder disorders and for the kidneys; in eye drops it helps with cataract."[20] The ancients often—but not always—suggested preparing these medical potions by infusing the plant materials in wine. *Materia Medica* also discusses three species of wormwood, including absinthium, maritime, and palmate, but recommends "true wormwood" *(Artemisia abrotanum)* in most cases, both internally and externally, as a diuretic and to relieve flatulence; and as an antidote to poison and even to drunkenness. Most significantly, however, is his claim that wormwood is an aphrodisiac and assists in sexual performance. Dioscorides also mentions a wine made with wormwood used by peoples of Propontis and Thrace, which they drink for all the mentioned purported health benefits.[21]

Pliny, on the other hand, set forth sixty-six different varieties of "artificial wines" (aromatized wines) that people were drinking, apparently for pleasure, without any suggestion that they had positive health benefits. Pliny described wines made from the ripe grain of millet, from fruit such as the palm (employed by the Parthians, Indians, and all countries of the East), from figs, Syrian carob, pears, apples, and pomegranates. Pliny also set forth the recipe for *myrtidanum*, a Greek aromatized wine made with the tender

An illustration from an Arabic translation of Dioscorides's
Materia Medica, showing the preparation of one of his
healing elixirs.

sprigs and wild berries of myrtle. Not to stop there, the Greeks (and also the Romans) used radish, asparagus, cunila, origanum, parsley seed, abrotonum, wild mint, rue, catmint, wild thyme, and horehound to flavor wines as well. Others made wine from the naphew turnip, and the roots of squills, and Gallic nard. Pliny gave recipes for sweet wine with calamus, scented rush, costus, Syrian nard, amomum, cassia, cinnamon, saffron, palm-dates, and foal-foot. Pliny also references "other kinds of herbs" and mentions wormwood wine, "made of Pontic wormwood in the proportion of one pound to forty sextarii of must, which is then boiled down until it is reduced to one third, or else of slips of wormwood put in wine."[22]

While commoners drank the above-mentioned aromatized wines for pleasure, the upper classes had the resources to make more elaborate concoctions. By way of limited example, King Mithridates of Pontus (northeastern Turkey 120–63 BCE) took a daily drink of *Mithridaticum,* which consisted of a truly staggering list of ingredients, including putchuk, sweet flag, St. John's Wort, gum, sagapenum, gum Arabic, orris, cardamom, anise, Celtic nard, gentian root, dried rose petals, poppy latex, parsley cassia, hartwort, darnel, long pepper, storax, castoreum, frankincense, hypocistis, myrrh, opopanax, tejpat leaf, nut-grass flower, terebinth resin, galbanum, candy carrot, spikenard, balsam of Mecca, shepherd's purse, rhubarb root, saffron, ginger, and cinnamon. All of these were ground and mixed into honey and then infused into wine.[23]

For the next several hundred years, there is little distinction between drinking herb-and-spice-infused wine for pleasure versus for health. While there clearly existed aromatized wines that appear to have been created to be enjoyed purely for pleasure, these wines nonetheless contained botanicals believed to have positive health benefits. Likewise, it was not uncommon for purported medicinal mixtures to contain herbs and spices often found in food and wine. Citizens of the Greek and Roman empires who were in the economic positions to consider such factors simply believed that they should strive for balance in their lives and that the way to achieve this balance (and avoid sickness) was to drink various herb-infused wines depending on a variety of factors such as the time of the year or different symptoms afflicting the citizen.

A HEALING ELIXIR

In the early fourteenth century Franciscan Friar John of Rupescissa had visions of the end of the world, where "evangelical men" would be called upon to combat the forces of the Antichrist. These spiritual soldiers, he believed, would need to be fortified by "heavenly" medicine, or "alchemical quintessence," which would provide the strength necessary to survive the apocalyptic ordeal. Friar John elaborated the traditional four elements could not be relied upon to preserve the body because they themselves are subject to decay. As a result, a "fifth element" was needed, and that the fifth element was the spirit of wine, or more specifically the alcohol produced through multiple distillations of wine. Friar John published his *Consideration of the Quintessence* (written immediately following the Black Death) and it led to the radical idea that distillation could perfect the medicinal virtues of any drug.

To state the obvious, this *aqua vitae* was an immediate hit. Its popularity was helped by a widespread belief that it was a cure-all. Not only could it cure "the palsy," "ring worms, and all spots of the face" and expel poisons, but it could also "sharpen the wit and restore the memory," and "make men merry and preserve youth." The spirit was also believed to be wholesome for the stomach, heart, and liver, as well as able to nourish the blood. Finally, the good Friar promoted its unique ability to bring a good smell and taste to any wine.

People living in Europe during the 1500s routinely suffered through arbitrary diseases and merciless chronic illnesses, which either quickly killed off their victims or, worse, lingered. It wasn't just the plague (which at the time referred to influenza, typhus, meningitis, smallpox, and other contagious diseases, in addition to the famous Bubonic variety) that kept citizens awake at night. There were also numerous nonlethal ailments to endure, such as skin rashes, sores, ulcers, and trauma-based injuries. As a result, many people turned to medical self-help manuals to shed light on these maladies and suggest home treatments.

The mid-sixteenth century saw the first translations of ancient texts, specifically of the Greek botanist Dioscorides, whose first-century manual on

Medieval friars preparing their distilled spirit, from Hieronymus
Brunschwig's *Liber de arte Distillandi de Compositis*.

pharmacology was published in Italian in 1544. This translation, which at the time appeared to unlock long forgotten secrets of the universe, would lead to an entire industry of purported "healers" who claimed to possess the forgotten keys to life and happiness. In many instances, these "secrets" were just republished recipes and ideas from this classic text. Indeed, just a few years later one of the Renaissance's best known "healers," Leonardo Fioravanti, began suggesting the Greek herbalist's treatment for hundreds of ailments. [24]

But it was Girolamo Ruscelli's 1555 book *New Secrets (Secreti Nuovi)*, published under the pseudonym of self-styled Reverend Master Alexis (Alessio) of Piedmont, that set the stage—ten years after the Dioscorides translation—for a growing belief in the power of herbs and spice infusions to ward off the plague and heal other maladies as well. Readers of the *New Secrets* were led to believe that Alessio was a monk, alchemist, and indefatigable searcher of secrets. *New Secrets* contained over a thousand treatments for illnesses (about the same number as found in *Materia Medica*) from mange to memory loss, with additional sections on skin diseases, eye injuries, teeth and gum disease, and intestinal worms.

Alessio also transcribed several versions of *Absinthium* or *Absinthium vinum*, noting their usefulness in treating various diseases. In fact, the earliest written description of wormwood wine in Italian is found in his book, which not coincidently was published a few years after *Materia Medica* was translated into Italian. Alessio "revealed" in his book that wormwood wine is typically made with 48 pints of must to one pound of wormwood, which was boiled down before adding 90 pints of must and another half pound of wormwood. This concoction was very bitter, and so his other recipes called for adding 3 or 4 ounces of wormwood, as well as 2 ounces each of Syrian nard, cinnamon, cassia, calamus, ginger-grass, and crushed date stone.[25]

Ruscelli also prescribed the following combination to ward off the plague: "mastic, incense [Frankincense] . . . myrtle, bay, rosemary, sage, elder, rasis, ginger, and pitch all pounded together and set upon the coles."[26] Another recipe lifted from the ancient text. For citizens of Italy who still believed in the Four Humors, rubbing sage on themselves to ward off the plague did not sound as futile as it does today.

As I mentioned above, Alessio de Piedmont wasn't really Alessio de Piedmont, but was Girolamo Ruscelli, a fact that came out when his posthumous tract *Secreti Nuovi* was published.[27] Whatever Alessio did for Italians, he did not significantly change anyone's drinking habits. One of Ruscelli's . . . er, Alessio's literary nemeses, attacked his reputation for dabbling in alchemy and magic:

Everyone knows that Ruscelli is a good for nothing scoundrel, a swindler, and a cheat. He's ignorant and full of vice. Not being successful at alchemy, the pedantic profession that teaches all the learning of an ass, he has the temerity to translate Plutarch's Lives from Greek (of which he hasn't any more knowledge than a magpie), the Bible from Hebrew (which he knows about as well as my dog), and after a thousand ridiculous charlatan's recipes, he has lowered himself to the art of the pimp and has crammed his house with all sorts of courtesans and glad-handing prostitutes begging for the bread that they can't earn by their own talents.[28]

Alessio has been described by other writers as one of the forefathers of vermouth. Despite *New Secrets* being in publication for almost 200 years before 1790, I have been unable to find any evidence that Alessio in any significant way affected how or what people drank during this time period. The most that could be said is that he assisted in propagating the myth surrounding wormwood and its purported healing qualities.

A SOCIAL BEVERAGE

While the Catalan theologian and physician Arnau de Vilanova warned against the misuses of wine and spices, he nevertheless recommended spiced wines to be taken after meals in winter because they would aid in digestion. (The issue was one of moderation.) In 1307 he published his own particular recipe for an aromatized fortified wine called "piment" (meaning spice) in his *Regimen sanitatis* ("Rules of Health"), which he recommended to his patients. A popular recipe for piment called for an ounce of cinnamon, ginger, a dram of cloves, nutmeg, lavender, long pepper, galangal, two drams of grains of paradise, and a half an ounce of black pepper, all pulverized with a mortar and pestle, and then soaked in two pounds of brandy that was distilled twice, and kept there for fifteen days. After straining off the botanicals, only three or four drops of this added to a bottle of good wine made a quality piment.[29]

While the belief in the health properties of herbs and spices continued, the divergence between aromatized wines for the banquet table and blends for pharmacies began to emerge by the mid-sixteenth century. In 1559 Peter Morwen translated into English from the Latin Conrad Gesner's *The Treasure of Euonymus*, which described an aromatized wine as "Vinum Raspoticum" or Rappis. Gesner defined "Raspish wine" as wine "which bite the tongue with a certain sharp biting, provoking the appetite, binding the heats of the stomach." He gave a recipe suggesting "galangal, five ounces, cinnamon, cloves, of either two drachms." This was not a medicinal drink, but one for pleasure.

In 1576, George Baker released yet another "translation" of *Treasure of Euonymus*, calling it *The Newe Jewell of Health*. In his book, Baker promoted not just the drinking of spirits straight, but concoctions of spirit, wine, aromatic plants, roots, spices, and seeds are lauded as "comfortable, commendable, and singular cordial wines." They were popular in England at this time. These drinks were prepared by infusing borrage, endives, ginger, long pepper, sage, galingale, cloves, fennel, and nutmeg. Some of these spirituous liquors were also made with the addition of sugar. Other aromatized wines, some with and some without the addition of fortifying spirits, were drunk before meals as aperitifs. A decade later, Michel de Montaigne, the sixteenth-century French author, published a piece entitled *Essais sur les Moeurs* (1588) that mentioned an "aqua composita," as made of strong wine without lees, and spices, or herbs, or roots, or all of these combined.[30] Clearly, fortified aromatized wines were being drunk for pleasure all over Europe by the late sixteenth century.

Food and drink during antiquity received considerable attention from the average citizen, and were at the heart of constant discussions about healthy living in what is now Western Europe. This interest is reflected in a panoply of recipe books and texts on food's interaction with the body, as well as in the growth of courtly dining and banqueting. Significantly, the only drinks mentioned in these early recipe books are water and wine; as of the early sixteenth century other beverages—specifically infusions of herbs and cordials—were still regarded as medicines. That wine was no longer fermented solely by apothecaries for medicinal purposes was relatively new, but by 1559, when Peter Morwen translated *Treasure of Euonymus*, wine had completed its transition from medicine to pleasure beverage. Aromatized wines were not far behind.[31]

Just what exactly had wealthy Romans been eating and drinking during the past two thousand years? While the sixteenth century saw an influx in republished recipes calling for various aromatized wines—often with recipes horrifyingly bitter and certainly not actually drunk by anyone—what the citizenry was actually drinking for pleasure was something quite different and new. Mediterranean peoples have long preferred rare, exotic, and purportedly impossible to obtain spices and aromatics over native spices. As soon as trade routes were established and spices such as cinnamon, pepper, ginger, cardamom, nutmeg, and vanilla became available, they found their way into wines.

MULSUM

One of the most popular aromatized wines during the Roman period went by the name *mulsum*, which was liberally flavored with myrrh. Myrrh was one of the rarest and most sought after spices during the time of Christ. Indeed, it was one of the gifts brought to the newborn Messiah by the three wise men (the others being gold and frankincense). Myrrh was involved in divine worship and human festivities among the Jewish, Greek, and Romans. Perhaps not coincidently, it was also the first example Theophrastus gave when discussing the spicing of wine, explaining that it wasn't just the perfume, but also its pungency and its heat.[32] Most significantly, perhaps, were its medicinal qualities, powers of "heating, soporific, sealing, drying, and astringent." But that wasn't all. Myrrh also "relaxes and opens the closed womb, and rapidly causes menstruation or abortion when applied with wormwood or the water from cooking lupin seeds or the juice of rue."[33] Lest you think myrrh was done after that, it was also mixed with cassia and honey and applied to the face for acne, or used with vinegar to clear sycosis. Rub it onto the head with laudanum, wine and myrtle wine and it would prevent baldness. Myrrh was also believed to heal sores in the eyes, cure white patches and blind spots in the pupils, and smooth away trachoma.[34]

With this kind of reputation, and during a period when there was no real distinction between food and drugs, mulsum (spiced honeyed wine) became a staple aperitif at Roman feasts. Some called it "Nectar," and it was made by simply placing Attic honey in an earthenware vessel set in hot ashes. Once the honey was heated, the maker could drive off the scum before adding wine and then transferring the mixture to resinated jars, which were hung in linen bags containing chopped putchuk. Adding tejpat leaf (another precious aromatic used in perfume, medicine, and cooking) was advised, but not essential. The mulsum was then aged for at least fifteen days, although it was well known that the longer it sat, the better the flavor. Another recipe called for adding myrrh, cassia, putchuk, spikenard, and pepper instead of the tejpat leaf, and then leaving it to stand in the sun "from the rise of the Dog Star for 40 days."[35]

CONDITUM

Mulsum fell out of fashion toward the end of the Roman Empire, as its citizenry turned its attention to the more modern *conditum,* which was not so much a single drink as an idea. The idea was that aromatized wine should be seasonal, not the same year round. For people who believed that the secret to human health was maintaining proper balance among the four humors, it would make sense to ensure that the spices (i.e., medication) in your wine changed with the seasons. Conditum spices were adjusted so that there was nothing too heating in summer, cooling in winter, or drying in spring. While conditum appears to have been drunk as a social beverage—its ingredients (pepper, mastic, tejpat leaf, saffron, and roasted dates) being relatively identical to mulsum—it also shows up in Byzantine medical texts.

A fourth-century recipe describes the process as requiring the maker to bring to a boil 15 pounds of honey and two pints of wine in a bronze jar over a slow fire of dry wood, while stirring constantly and adding additional wine as the mixture boils over. The following day, after the sweetened wine was skimmed, the recipe called for adding pepper, mastic, tejpat leaf, and saffron, as well as roasted date stones and the flesh of dates that had been previously softened in wine. This aromatized wine concentrate was then added to smooth wine. Any remaining bitter flavors were corrected with the use of coal.[36]

HIPPOCRAS

By the medieval period, however, all of these drinks were resigned to the dustbin of history. The brand-new favorite was called *hippocras,* and it caught on like wildfire because the drink was delicious. Hippocras (or ipocras or ypocras) was also supposedly good for your health, but by this time, the health part was a bit of an afterthought. It was believed to be an aphrodisiac too, so between purported health benefits, effect on sexuality, and the taste, there was simply no reason not to drink it. While the name of the drink was meant to pay homage to Hippocrates, the father of medicine, this appears to be a nod in his direction rather than an actual statement on its medicinal properties.

Hippocras was originally reserved for the nobility, but eventually it filtered down to the upper classes once sugar became more affordable. At first hippocras was part of a very showy dessert course, and it later became the ceremonial drink at Dutch weddings.[37] Medieval meals (for the comfortable classes anyway) always included a spiced wine served both before and after a meal. For example, a celebration given in 1458 by the Count of Foix (in the foothills of the French Pyrenees) for envoys from Hungary started with an aperitif of white hippocras, and finished with a digestif of red hippocras. According to academic Kirstin Kennedy, "the Flemish courtier Antoine de Lalaing, who accompanied Philip the Fair on his visit to Spain in 1501, recorded that in Navarre it was the custom after a tournament to present wine and spices to the watching ladies."[38]

During the fifteenth century, there were two kinds of hippocras, the expensive kind and the cheap kind. You can guess who drank which. The expensive kind required five spices: sugar, cinnamon, ginger, grains of paradise, and turnsole. Each of these ingredients was prohibitively expensive in medieval Europe, particularly sugar, which was considered as exotic as cinnamon from Sri Lanka and ginger from China. Sugar was the best-known and most effective sweetener in the Roman world and, like all other spices, was believed to be a medicine, in this case a laxative used for bladder and kidney disorders or an eye drop used for treating cataracts. It also was believed to "increase the semen," which may explain why I drank my coffee black and unsweetened throughout college. The cheaper version of hippocras used substitutions for each ingredient, except ginger, which couldn't be easily imitated. But it was made more often than not using honey instead of sugar, cassia instead of cinnamon, long pepper instead of grains of paradise, and sunflower instead of turnsole. This was the telltale sign of the cheaper stuff, as turnsole had a radiant blue-purple coloring that sunflower could not replicate.

The quantities necessary for good hippocras suggest an ounce of cinnamon, two ounces of ginger, one pound of sugar, twenty cloves, and twenty peppercorns soaked in a gallon of wine, and strained through a conical cloth filter bag

Still Life of Glass, Pottery, and Sweets, Juan van der Hamen, 1622.

called a *manicum hippocraticum* or Hippocratic sleeve (originally devised by Hippocrates to filter water).

Notwithstanding the pleasurable aspect of drinking aromatized wines, the *Encyclopedia Britannica* as late as 1823 defines hippocras as "a medicinal drink, composed of wine, with spices, and other ingredients infused therein; much used among the French by way of a cordial dram after meals." There are a number of different kinds of hippocras, varying according to the kind of wine and other additional ingredients used: white hippocras, red hippocras, claret hippocras, strawberry hippocras, absinthe hippocras, cider hippocras, etc. Recipes from the late London Dispensary were to be made of cloves, ginger, cinnamon, and nutmeg, beat and infused in canary wine (a popular 16th century fortified wine from the Canary Islands, similar to Madeira) with sugar; to the infusion, milk, a lemon, and some slips of rosemary were added and the whole strained through a funnel. It was recommended as a cordial, though it could also be used in paralytic and other nervous cases.[39]

Another recipe for hippocras, or *Vinum Hippocraticum*, called for a quart of white wine, set over a low fire, to which eight quarts of virgin honey were added, then roasted dates pressed to a paste, plus a sweat leaf called folium, ground pepper, and a pinch of saffron. Two more gallons of wine went in, until the liquor's thickness could bear an egg, and then cloves and mace tied up in a hippocras sack were steeped in the liquor.[40] Hippocras and clarre were made in great variety, either with spices alone or with spices and honey or sugar, and both enjoyed an ancient, solid reputation.[41] At the christening of Prince Edward, everyone was served with this sweet wine.[42]

This focus on Hippocras shouldn't suggest that there were only a few recipes for aromatized and flavored wines. Quite the contrary. Banquet dining almost always ended with a flavored wine course and the recipes were limitless. Not only were the traditional hippocras botanicals added to wine, but any number of herbs and spices such as citron, cloves, myrtle, cypress leaves, southernwood, asparagus flowers and fenugreek were also used.[43] Additional recipes called for peach leaves or coriander, goats' horns, or clary sage. Horminum was used to give the wine a musky odor that was popular with the Germans. Other recipes called for almonds, raisins, olive pits, pine resin, orris root, spikenard, *Artemisia*, and myrrh. Obviously, the rare medieval spices such as zedoary, long pepper, grains of paradise, galangal, mastic, and camphor were highly prized.

Art is another historical source for what was actually being drunk. The Continental banquet course was captured in several well-known paintings that offer terrific insight into culinary trends during the seventeenth century. Clara Peeters' *Still Life with Flowers, Goblet, Dried Fruit, and Pretzels* (1611) portrays a wine goblet on a table with a variety of nuts, confectionaries, and biscuits (hence the phrase "from soup to nuts," which references something being complete, as meals started with soup). Juan van der Hamen's *Still Life of Glass, Pottery, and Sweets* (1622) portrays hippocras and wafers, which were the main components of the medieval banquet, from which the early modern wine and sweetmeats course originated.[44] The French referred to this end of meal ritual as the *voidée* or void, which was a glass of wine with spices after the tables had been cleared.

Of course, hippocras eventually fell out of flavor, and the overly sugared and spiced profile appeared out of sync with evolving palates. Indeed, Madame Bovary, the woman whom Gustave Flaubert brought to life in 1857 (also bringing literature into modernity), referred to hippocras while describing Madame Homais's desire for heavy bread rolls as "the last surviving relics of Gothic fare, dating back, perhaps to the Crusades, and upon which in past ages, the lusty Normans used to gorge themselves, imagining that before them on the table, lit by the yellow glow of torches and flanked by flagons of hippocras and giant slabs of salted pork."[45]

WERMUT (VERMOUTH)

Given the high price and the ever increasing perceived value of spices in Europe, there was significant effort expended during the sixteenth and seventeenth centuries on figuring out how to obtain spices without paying the hefty price tags. The Venetians had controlled the spice trade out of Constantinople since 1204, when they sacked and pillaged the city during the Fourth Crusade. Genoese retailers who purchased from Arab merchants were also able to command high prices in Europe. This led to the Portuguese "discovering" that awfully helpful route East around the Cape of Good Hope, where they were able to purchases spices direct from producers at prices that made them giggle with joy. The Spanish, as we know, set out for the west and brought an entirely new crop of spices back from the New World. As a result of these explorations, the price of spices dropped like a hammer into a lake. Spices went from being a sign of wealth, used by the rich in food,

Still Life with Flowers, Goblet, Dried Fruit, and Pretzels, Clara Peeters, 1611.

wine, and perfumes, to being accessible to practically everyone and used for everything under the sun, including new inventions such as the scented glove and aromatic liqueurs.

By the time Italian distiller Antonio Benedetto Carpano was toiling away as a wine-shop assistant in Turin in the late eighteeth century, the entire world's spice supply could be found at his doorstep at prices that allowed for abundant use. Whereas prior aromatic wines such as mulsum, conditum, and hippocras usually contained five or fewer different spices, Carpano had

The Medicinal Properties of Wormwood

Does wormwood have actual medical properties? To answer this, one must break wormwood down into its chemical components. As it turns out, this was done in the early twentieth century when absinthe was all the rage and wormwood was being blamed for Van Gogh slicing off his ear.

While *A. absinthium* (and mugwort) has been used since ancient times for its purported healing properties, in 2006, an esteemed group of scientists from Serbia and Montenegro set out to investigate the specific chemical components of its essential oil, using chemotypes of *A. absinthium* and *A. vulgaris* from Serbia.[47] Much press has focused on what was believed to be the only active ingredient in *Artemisia*, thujone (pronounced thoo-joan). Thujone is a ketone and a monoterpene that occurs naturally in two forms: (−)-α-(+)-β-thujone. It has a menthol odor in its pure form.

The Serbian study broke down the *Artemisia* into literally hundreds of chemical components, and found, as believed, that thujone was a major, but not isolated, relevant chemical compound. As expected, differences were found in the roots and the leaves, with no thujone being found in the root of *A. absinthium*. Another factor accounting for a wide spectrum in thujone content was where geographically the *A. absinthium* was harvested.

The researchers found that both thujone isomers showed "high antimicrobial activity," particularly against E. coli. The findings went so far as to suggest that "it can be concluded that the antimicrobial activity in some of the analyzed flavor compounds . . . is comparable with those of well-known antibiotics, such as erythromycin."

Artemisia [1—4. Blüthe 5—7. Saame] Beyfuß.

The researchers declined to suggest its use in the same way because of self-dosage limitations, and because of prior findings, which suggest that extremely high doses of thujone can lead to nervous system toxicity, seizures, and death. In plain English, seven thousand years later we know what the rulers in the Shang Dynasty knew: that various species of *Artemisia*, if taken in the right doses, have some positive health benefits.

It is the thujone that is responsible for the antimicrobial activity. Thujone, of course, is found not only in *Artemisia*, but in various other plants as well, including arborvitae, junipers, mugwort, oregano, tansy, and various mints, as well as common sage. Indeed, sage has a higher thujone content than any species of *Artemisia*, by a significant amount. Science suggests that the thujone isomers in *Artemisia* are identical to the thujone in these other plants as well. Both United States and EU law severely restrict the use of thujone in vermouth. As a result, producers who use wormwood in their vermouth must either use a minimal amount, or extract the thujone from the wormwood prior to its use.

Artemisia absinthium from Franz Köhler's *Medicinal Plants.*

VERMOUTH

the luxury of creating one with over thirty (perhaps even fifty!) thanks to the military and strategic success of his government. There is no real distinction between 1786 Carpano's elixir and the previous ones being served on banquet dining tables, other than the sheer complexity of flavors created by the numerous amounts of distinct plant flavorings added. At no time in history would such a lavish infusion have been attempted for sale to the general population, as it would have been prohibitively expensive. It was the first vermouth, or, as he called it, "wermut."

Something else was happening during this time, too. Italians were studying their own history and uncovering long forgotten beverages enjoyed by their Roman ancestors. Italian writer C. Villifranchi published *Tuscan Oenology* in 1773, and it was one of the first times an Italian writer described the ancient Romans' drink, *Absinthiatum* or *Absinthiatum vinum*.[46] In *Tuscan Oenology*, Villifranchi revealed a recipe first published in Pliny the Elder's *Natural History*, as well as recipes from Dioscorides' *Materia Medica*. Villifranchi suggested that *Absinthiatum vinum* was in existence since the first century of the Christian era, though later evidence demonstrates that no one was actually producing or drinking this beverage on any scale in the mid-1700s. That being said, Villifranchi wrote, in 1773, thirteen years before Carpano released his "wermut," that he also believed that the word "vermouth" was German, noting that there is a white wine there that is good for digestion, and that some have figured out how to make one that is a "culinary delicacy."

Recipes for *Absinthium vinum* were also widely published in English by this time. *The Complete Dictionary of Arts and Sciences* (1766) notes that "several medicinal compositions are prepared from this plant; and, among others, the absinthiues vinum, or wormwood wine."[48]

The recipe is then given: "To make wormwood wine, take four pounds of the tops of each of [*Absinthium vulgare*, or common wormwood], when fresh and in bloom, clean, and either mince or bruise them, then put them together, with three drams of powdered cinnamon, into a barrel which will contain fifty quarts, fill the barrel with must from expressed white grapes, and leave the barrel into a cellar, leaving the wine to ferment." When the fermentation was over, the recipe instructed the reader to "fill up the cask with white wine, bottle it, and keep it for use."

Then, Nicolas Culpepper, a foremost astrologer, physician, and botanist, did his share of promoting the purported health benefits of *Artemisia absinthium,* by publishing in the 1780 edition of *The English Physician*—six years before Carpano created his Wermut—claims that wormwood could cure just about everything from cholera to impotence, in addition to being the antidote to rat and mice bites (think the plague) as well as to poisonous mushrooms, and that it could take away the pain from wasp, hornet, and scorpion stings.

Most helpful, perhaps, was wormwood's usefulness in "freeing virgins from the scab, curing melancholy in old men, making covetous men splenetic, curing the right eye of a man and the left eye of a woman . . . curing both spleen and liver, preventing drunkenness, and most importantly, preventing [syphilis]."

What this means is that while Carpano was working as a lowly sales associate in his wine shop across the street from the Royal Palace, two things were happening: the price of exotic spices from faraway lands were becoming incredibly cheap, and an abundant shrub found in mountain hillsides near where he lived was being touted as a panacea. To help matters, this panacea was also referenced in newly republished recipes from ancient medical and pharmacology texts, and it was rumored to be capable of producing a culinary delicacy when made properly.

What did Carpano do with this rich tapestry of circumstance? According to the Carpano company:

Sporting a comfortable paunch (thought of in his day as a sign of wisdom and affability), he wore a smart white waistcoat under a tan overcoat, and short breeches over his tight fitting hose. For years, our inventor toiled in his laboratory, mixing herbs and spices, boiling, macerating and perfecting his formula, which has not yielded its secret to this present day. To this mixture he added a light, white wine from the surrounding hills and after trying it himself pronounced it perfect; only then did he offer a glass to his beloved.

The company goes on to give hints about his recipe:

How many different herbs go to make up Antonio Benedetto Carpano's famous secret recipe? There are reputed to be over fifty and probably only one person can name them all.[49]

In the end, he called his creation "Wermut," which is best described as a next generation hippocras, with increased complexity due to the large amount of botanicals used. The Italian publication *Vini Italia* has described Vinum Hippocraticum as a prototype of vermouth de Turin.[50] Most importantly, he was able to sell it at a price that enabled the bourgeois and merchant classes to purchase it, so much so that the company reports that the wine shop stayed opened twenty-four hours a day. The wine shop became Turin's favorite bar and meeting place and remained the center of Turinese social life for years.

Even if Carpano wasn't the first person to combine dozens of aromatics in wine with brandy, he used a higher quality wine and perfected a drink that hit upon the two most popular flavors at the time: sweet and bitter. The practice, in theory and in limited amounts, may have been kicking around for at least two hundred years (Piment had brandy, wine, and aromatics in the 1500s), but he did commercialize it, and that is worthy of our admiration. The industry grew quickly, with new commercial producers coming onto the market within the next several decades, many of which are still known today, such as Noilly Prat and Cinzano. It was an industry that eventually changed how much of the world drank.

Did Carpano Really Invent Vermouth?

At the Portland Oregon Spirits festival in the fall of 2014, Cinzano rocked the world of vermouth by stepping forward and suggesting that Cinzano, not Carpano, invented "vermouth," claiming that they had produced an aromatized fortified wine in 1757, eleven years before Carpano. Is there any truth to this contention?

Not that I could find. In 1707, Giovanni Cinzano became a member of the confectioners and distillers guild when he got his license from the Duke of Savoy to distill brandy and cordials for sale in Turin and in his own village of Pecetto. In 1757, the Cinzano brothers, Giovanni Giacamo Cinzano and Carlo Stefano Cinzano, were admitted to the University of Confectioners and Spirits Manufacturers in the Italian City of Turin. I have not seen any evidence suggesting that they created "vermouth" in that year, or at anytime earlier than the nineteenth century. Indeed, in the Official Catalogue to the Dublin International Exhibition, 1865, the description of Cinzano states that "This house was established in 1814 by the father of the exhibitor and conducted until 1850 by Francesco Cinzano." So while, Cinzano may have gotten a distiller's license in that year, it does not appear it was a vermouth house at that time, or for the next fifty years. This is consistent with Cinzano advertising campaign in the United States during the 1940s, when its ads in *LIFE* magazine noted that Cinzano can be found all around the world, and "Since the day—over a century ago—when a member of the Cinzano family first came upon its magic formula—this magnificent vermouth has spread to the four corners of the earth."[51] If, in fact, Cinzano vermouth was first created in 1757, it is likely the company would have been promoting its two-century heritage, not its one-century history.

THE COCKTAIL

As early as 1869, Haney's *Steward and Barkeeper's Manual* published the first Old Fashioned "Vermuth Cocktail." It was and remains the perfect way to enjoy a glass of vermouth. Just be certain to use a brand that produces vermouth intended to be drunk on its own, as opposed to formulated for mixing.* "One wine glass of vermouth; one very small piece of ice; one small piece of lemon peel. Serve in a thin stemmed wine glass with curved lip."

This is exactly how Sother Teague, the head bartender of Amor Y Amargo, America's premier vermouth and bitters bar in the Lower East Side of New York City, suggests making it today, in 2015. His only adjustment is to do away with the ice and lemon peel: simply "pour it out of the bottle and drink it." It is unsurprising, therefore, that the Vermouth Cocktail, along with the Manhattan, Martini, and Old Fashioned was listed as the "famous cocktails that the public called for" at the historic Hoffmann House.[52]

Over the next twenty years after this recipe was first published, when vermouth began to hit its stride as the most important cocktail ingredient, every single notable mixologist put their own individual fingerprint on this drink. Indeed, in the same way that the true test of a chef is how they can cook an egg, bartenders each needed to be able to create an individualized vermouth cocktail.

Harry Johnson, in his heralded *The New and Improved Illustrated Bartender's Manual; Or: How to Mix Drinks* (1882), suggested making a Vermouth Cocktail by filling a wine glass with vermouth, adding four or five dashes of "gum" (simple syrup); two or three dashes of bitters (Boker's genuine only) and two dashes of Maraschino. He suggested you "stir up well with a spoon; strain it into a cocktail glass, twist a piece of lemon peel on top, and serve."

The following year, barman P. McDonough did away with the bitters and cut back on the simple syrup; he suggested adding just a few dashes of syrup to a

---

*   While there is an absence of any cocktails containing vermouth in the 1862 first printing of Jerry Thomas's *How to Mix Drinks: or the Bon Vivant's Companion* (which only included thirteen cocktails in total), it did include over a dozen recipes for vermouth's closest relative, Hippocras.

The dining room at New York City's famed Hoffman House.

pony-wine-glass of Vermouth. The Only William made his with a dash of bitters, two dashes of Maraschino and a dash of absinthe. The Only William was also the only one who stirred his to the freezing point. George J. Kappeler made his vermouth cocktail with two dashes of Angostura or Peychaud's bitters and would garnish it with a cherry. He also was one of the first to suggest a French vermouth cocktail that used a couple dashes of orange bitters.

All of these are still excellent ways to make a vermouth cocktail. But with so many excellent liqueurs on the market and easily accessible, the possibilities are now limitless.

ROCKS   WINE

THE VERMOUTH COCKTAIL

INGREDIENTS

3 oz. dry or sweet vermouth

INSTRUCTIONS

Pour vermouth straight out of the bottle directly into a wine glass or rocks glass. Serve either chilled or on the rocks. Garnish to your taste.
I recommend a slice of lemon for dry vermouths, a slice or orange or a cherry for sweeter styles.

The simplest cocktails are sometimes the best. The Vermouth Cocktail is just what it sounds like: Vermouth straight poured, either chilled or on the rocks, perhaps with a dash of Maraschino or absinthe (or both). Add a twist of lemon, or an olive, or a piece of seasonal fruit.

If this sounds like a drink that you can just pour and personalize to your liking, you're right. There is no right or wrong answer. Real vermouth is meant to be (1) drunk straight and (2) enjoyed any way you like.

chapter two

VERMOUTH IN AMERICA

For the past 150 years, vermouth has shaped cocktail culture in the United States more than any other spirit. America's cocktail culture would not have evolved in the manner it did without this enigmatic, aromatized, and fortified wine. While a handful of simple cocktails existed prior to vermouth reaching American shores in earnest in the 1850s and '60s, these drinks were primitive, rustic, harsh affairs, lacking the complexity and balance and deliciousness that we have all now come to expect in a properly mixed drink.

Sure, people were having their punches, crustas, slings, and whatnot in the nineteenth century, but sophistication and elegance did not reach the cocktail glass until vermouth arrived and the quintessential Manhattan and Martini—the two greatest (and most longstanding) cocktails—were invented. Vermouth spent almost a century as the primary ingredient of these two drinks. Yes, the Martini and the Manhattan both originally called for *two parts vermouth to one part gin or whiskey.* (A far cry from the whisper of vermouth swished over the cocktail glass for the past three generations!) And from at least the 1880s through the 1950s, these were pretty much the only two cocktails that Americans were drinking in serious quantities.

Even when the heavy use of vermouth in cocktails fell out of fashion post–World War II, vermouth still managed to stay firmly entrenched in our collective conscience. Unshakable. Unforgettable. While the Drapers and Sterlings may have been asking since the 1940s for Martinis and Manhattans increasingly drier (meaning with less and less vermouth)—drier to the point of infinity—Americans would acknowledge that vermouth is what you're *supposed to* put in these drinks, even if you choose not to, because that was *de rigueur* for the time. In other words, even when vermouth wasn't there, it has always been there—like a good lover you haven't seen for twenty years.

Indeed, as we'll discover, the level of collective angst and sadness in American history is inversely proportional to the amount of vermouth we were drinking at that time. But enough with the grand abstractions; let's take the first-ever granular look into vermouth's history in the United States.

In the previous chapter we discussed vermouth's Chinese, Persian, and Mediterranean history. However, the ancient art and science of adding herbs and spices to wine and other fermented beverages was not limited to those regions, but extended to the Americas as well. In South America, the archeological evidence points directly at early humans—who crossed over the Bering land bridge around 20,000 years ago—as having experimented with and later perfected the same type of medicinal wine that the Chinese, Indians, Egyptians, Persians, and Europeans were drinking at roughly the same time. Archeological excavations throughout the Andes, Amazonia, and southern Mexico demonstrate that these peoples also steeped "medicinal" herbs such as tree resins (which can produce a sherry-like fragrance), chili peppers, and vanilla into various fermented beverages made of either honey, cacao pods, or fruits. These beverages were then incorporated into ceremonies and enjoyed socially, just as they were elsewhere.

The practice of infusing wine with herbs, roots, barks, and spices didn't, however, find its way to indigenous North Americans. Despite the existence of more wild grape varieties in North America (twenty to twenty-five unique species) than anywhere else in the world, there is no "decisive archaeological or chemical evidence to demonstrate that native peoples [in North America] collected grapes for food, let alone . . . made wine from its fruit."[53] The reason why is unknown, but the best hypothesis, given by Patrick McGovern, is simply that the indigenous peoples who settled in North America came from Siberia, a location short on any high-sugar resources necessary to create alcohol, and as a result evolved lacking the ability to process alcohol.[54] Indeed, prior to the arrival of Europeans, Native Americans lived happily without alcohol (tobacco and psychedelic mushrooms were their drugs of choice).

Europeans settlers in America, on the other hand, were drinking something we would easily categorize as vermouth well before the Revolutionary War in 1776. (Ten years before Antonio Benedetto Carpano created his commercial version in Turin and named it "wermut.") During the war it was a popular (and rarely contradicted) belief that soldiers needed alcohol to keep in shape.[55] One of history's little known facts is that while rebelling against the Red Coats, our undisciplined, rag-tag American soldiers were drinking vermouth's predecessor. Unsurprisingly, it was one of Britain's choice beverages: Purl-Royal. Purl-Royal was a sweet sherry that had been infused with dozens of medicinal botanicals such as dates, dill, saffron, nigella seeds, hazelwort, juniper, and its dominant flavoring agent, gentian, then fortified with brandy. The product was exported from Britain under the branded name Dr. Stoughton's Elixir Magnum Stomachicum. Stoughton had been making this medicinal cordial for twenty years before receiving a patent on it, on the claim that its secret mixture of twenty-two botanicals could cure any stomach ailment, cleanse the blood of any impurities, and take care of scurvy.[56] While Stoughton's Elixir was not sold to the general public as a social, pleasurable drink but rather as a medicine, during the war years it was perfectly acceptable to take the concentrated Stoughton's Cordial Elixir and mix it with natural wine, thus making it more enjoyable. In other words, American revolutionary soldiers were creating homemade vermouth, at least ten years before it was called "vermouth."

Americans, of course, are good at taking ideas and improving upon them with good old-fashioned American ingenuity, creativity, and stubbornness, so it is not surprising that colonists became quite adept at using the various barks, herbs, and roots they found in abundance in pre-industrial American forests to make elixirs, and that they then added those mixtures to their glasses of wine. They called it "native" wine or "spiced" wine.

While sparse records suggest that early American settlers were making something approximating vermouth for personal use, there are not any written

CONTRATTO

records of Americans commercially producing aromatized fortified wines prior to the end of the nineteenth century. Commercial European vermouths, however, were available (although in extremely limited places and quantities) in the United States since perhaps 1836. Not much is known about who was drinking which vermouth for the next two decades, although world-renowned cocktail historian David Wondrich speculates that it was "miners and whores."[57] (Records suggest vermouth was shipped to San Francisco during the gold rush, a time during which that city was long on both those categories of individual.) Wondrich's hypothesis might be true, but even if it's not, I can't think of a more vivid description of potential nineteenth century drinkers, so I'll let it be.

Whether or not Americans were drinking Italian or French commercial vermouth in the 1850s, it's fair to say that it was a bit of a novelty in America, until at least the 1860s. Very little is written about vermouth before then. And although we see some receipts of shipments coming in to American shores, these early shipments do not appear to immediately make their way into the bartender's toolbox. Rather, most of what was first imported was originally sold to apothecary shops, where it was considered to be, and was resold as, a medicine like Stoughton's Elixir had been considered in the prior century. Indeed, as a trip to the Syracuse apothecary museum (nestled inside the Children's Museum of Art and Science) will reveal, throughout the middle nineteenth century it was standard practice for pharmacists to infuse medicinal plants in wine and alcohol, which was then ingested to purportedly cure various diseases. The Venn diagram between wine with herbs and brandy that were drunk for pleasure as opposed to because they were good for you was still overlapping in America of the 1860s and 1870s. As a result, vermouth continues to show up in pharmaceutical journals as late as 1899, by which time the pharmacists were leveraging the drink's newfound popularity to sell their own herb-infused wine concoctions.

The story of vermouth in the United States gets interesting in New York City in the 1870s. But the seed is planted in 1853, so it's worth taking a step back a couple of decades to set the stage. By the middle of the nineteenth century, New York City had solidified as the most important port city in America, and it sought to further entrench its dominance as the premier commercial, financial, mercantile and industrial city in the New World. In furtherance of this, it played host to *The Exhibition of the Industry of All Nations*—a World's Fair. It was the first World's Fair to take place on U.S. soil and was stunning in presentation, scope, and success. It took place on present day Bryant Park (40th to 42nd Streets between 5th and 6th Avenues in midtown Manhattan). The action happened inside the Crystal Palace, a 123-foot-high glass dome structure whose construction involved 1,800 tons of steel and 15,000 panes of glass. To put this glitzy building in perspective, it was the tallest building in all of the Americas at the time. It would be another twenty-five years until the Tribune building became New York's first skyscraper, which stood 260 feet—a mere nine stories. The Crystal Palace proclaimed, in no uncertain terms, that New York had arrived.

The Crystal Palace hosted over 4,390 exhibitors, and just about every single New Yorker visited the event at least once, Walt Whitman and Mark Twain included. It was here, in the midst of the animals and agriculture, that representatives from four largely unknown Italian companies poured the most peculiar beverages. They were listed as "vermout" on the playbill. These drinks, ever so slightly different in overall mouthfeel and flavor to one another, were all completely different from anything else the attendees had ever tasted. Charles Dickens described them as "at first slightly bitter and afterwards sweet, reminding one rather of the orange peel in syrup in good home-made marmalade."[58] The four European producers in attendance were M. Bovone, G&L Cora, Giuseppe Carpano (Antonio Benedetto Carpano's nephew, who took over the company after his death), and the Dettoni Brothers.[59]

These four producers do not appear to have made a huge splash at this event. Given Giuseppe's bloodline as a direct relative of the first commercial producers of vermouth, he may have been expected to be treated like royalty, but it is simply not possible to show up with a completely new category of alcoholic beverage and expect New Yorkers to immediately fall in love with it, or even lust after it.

And indeed, it doesn't appear that New Yorkers did. Or if they did, the historical record has failed to capture it. There was no immediate fascination with

The exterior of New York's Crystal Palace at the World's Fair in 1853.

aromatized and fortified wine. Like any good love story, it took the right mix of history, serendipity, and timing.

NEW YORK IN THE CIVIL WAR

Ten years later, the timing greatly improved. Civil War–era Manhattan provided that perfect mix, that necessary confluence that allowed for these Italian vermouths to bring social drinking out of the stone ages and into modernity.

New York City in the 1860s has long been described as a dichotomous town. It was a "semi-barbarous metropolis" that was "half as luxurious and artistic as Paris" and half as "savage as Cairo or Constantinople."[60] The city was categorized as being split into two realms: one of squalor and the other splendor. Writers at the time tripped over themselves to pen perfect alliterations when describing the polarity of the city: magnificence and mud, finery and filth, diamonds and dirt.[61]

On one hand, the city was filled with filth. New York had "entered upon a unparalleled era of wickedness"[62] in which the police could not enforce respect for the law, and the criminal element reveled in an "orgy of vice and crime."[63] Squalid tenement houses overflowed with impoverished immigrants. Those who could find work did so under horrifying conditions. Girls sewing umbrellas for eighteen hours a day earned just three dollars a week.[64] There were con artists and scammers, thieves and longshoremen who fought and fucked and drank nothing more than whiskey, sugar, and bitters, and then stole and fought some more. (Not necessarily in that order.) Muggings were common, and the more modern thieves would use knockout drops—chloral hydrate or morphine rags smothered on the victim's face—rather than a blackjack to the back of the head. Prostitutes "perched about the windows, stoops and cellar doors, like buzzards on dead trees."[65] It was not a place for the dainty.

These hardships are not surprising given the population changes happening in New York at the time. The city was in the midst of a human migration surge unlike any prior one in history. In 1855, New York City had 630,000 people (only about one third of them were gainfully employed).[66] By 1860, the number rose to 850,000, a

At right: An artist's rendering of the inside of the Crystal Palace exhibition.

33 percent increase. That would be like present day New York City going from eight million people to twelve million by 2018. Put another way, in 1854 the United States welcomed 428,000 immigrants, 319,000 of whom stayed in New York City. By 1855 over half of the city's residents were from outside the United States: 176,000 from Ireland, 98,000 from Germany, and 37,000 from England, Wales, or Scotland. Between 1865 and 1873, over two hundred thousand more arrived in NYC each year. Many were foreigners, but country folks were also forced to move from rural areas that provided little economic reward. So the city was bursting at the seams with the jobless and the destitute; low-paid newsboys, peddlers, apple sellers and hot-corn girls were practically stacked on top of one another.

But recall this town had two sides. On the other side of the New York coin was a Golden Age. As with any migration boom, there was a huge influx of courageous, savvy folks that also brought about a flood of wealth. The city was just as overflowing with bankers, brokers, importers, exporters, manufacturers, insurance tycoons, blueblood professionals, railroad barons, and the like. Women would attend parties draped in thousand dollar gowns. Over 122 individuals reported a net worth of more than $10,000 in 1856 (about 100 times more than the average annual income), and prosperous young New Yorkers learned how to live in luxury in ways that no prior generation had known. These were the "sporting men," as they were described in the press at that time. They owned horse-drawn carriages and put considerable effort into decorating their homes, deciding what style of clothes to wear, and of course, choosing what to eat and drink. For some, it was a time of unprecedented refinement and elegance.

Although often forgotten—or simply not discussed because they are much more difficult to describe and don't excite the same emotions as the downtrodden or the rich—a new group of citizens was also making their home in Civil War–era New York City: a middle class. I may get assaulted for breaking with the universal description of New York as a tale of two polar-opposite cities, but it happens to be true that a large class existed between these poles. Doctors, lawyers, accountants, merchants, and other professionals existed in the middle of New York's often over-emphasized extremes. And these individuals, like the super wealthy, also sought to live a life filled with the materials that had recently become available to them. Despite the lack of electricity, these citizens saw all that the city had to offer and wanted to reach in and take it all with both hands. They wanted not just a life, but a nightlife.

Prior to the 1860s, drinking, when done publicly, often took place in murky and raucous taverns or beer gardens. Most (though not all) of these were tough joints that hosted day laborers, cartmen, stevedores, and sailors. Women weren't particularly welcome in most of these establishments, and there wasn't much to do there except pound ales and lagers. And then maybe start a fistfight or shank someone. But New York's new middle and upper classes were looking for more refined places to spend their money and their evenings. They wished to drink in different surroundings.

Let's not avert our gaze from the other historical stream that leads to vermouth being the talk of the town. New Yorkers, both male and female, enjoyed and had a lot of sex in the 1860s. While those who lived in the woods outside the city were aghast at New Yorkers' ability to be intimate with multiple partners, sex and prostitution in town was just another ordinary facet of life. In 1855, a city directory contains sixty-nine women who listed themselves as "prostitutes."[67] Walt Whitman once commented that nineteen of every twenty males—including the best classes of men in Brooklyn and New York—visited brothels regularly. Indeed, the brothels located south of Houston were stylish affairs, run by entrepreneurial madams and noted for the attractiveness of the women, the luxurious furniture, finest liquor, and servants who doubled as piano players. This isn't to say that the commercial sex trade was all giggles and glamour. The gas-lit basement dives at the lower end of Bowery, in the Five Points, or along the waterfront were places you wouldn't have found Walt Whitman or the "best class of Men." And in some joints, greedy madams would overwork their girls, putting quotas on them, which resulted in an average of seventy to a hundred encounters a week.[68] Of course, at two dollars for fifteen minutes, these women were making hundreds of times what other working women were making at the time. (Seamstresses made three dollars a week, minus the cost of needles and thread.)[69]

It is against this backdrop that a new venue for nightlife emerged in New York. In 1860, a gentleman from Philadelphia moved to New York City and opened up the first "concert saloon," the Melodeon, in one of the old Assembly Theaters on Broadway (at Spring Street). This venue differentiated itself from the beer halls in that it combined music, drink, and sex all under one roof. The entertainment was a potpourri of vaudeville, Italian opera, German beer garden, and English theater. The idea, obviously, was to appeal to a wide variety of New Yorkers. The entertainers sang, and the audience joined in with tipsy vocals.

The concert saloon owners had a feel for the fabric of the time, and aimed to create a perfect evening for those looking for a night out on the town. They employed "waiter-girls" who often wore low bodices, short skirts, and high tasseled red boots (the original Hooters, one might say). These women sold drinks and, between acts, took a seat in the audience to sell themselves. Most concert saloons featured alcoves for the waiter girls and the customers to quickly get some privacy.

In the early 1860s, the majority of these concert saloons were concentrated on Broadway, south of Houston. By 1864, the stretch of Broadway between Houston and Prince Streets was the liveliest part of Manhattan, both indoors and outdoors.[70] The most famous concert saloon—not just in New York but in the United States—was Harry Hill's on Houston, just east of Broadway, two blocks north of the original Melodeon, one block south of Professor Jerry Thomas's Palace Bar at 622 Broadway. Harry's set the bar for concert saloons; its regulars included judges, lawyers, merchants, congressmen, and state legislators.

What makes these concert saloons so integral to the history of vermouth, however, is that they were filled with citizenry looking for a more modern drink than mere whiskey or beer. They employed professional bartenders who understood balance and lived their lives with the sole objective of creating perfect drinks for their customers. There was no higher compliment for such men than being called a "Broadway Bartender." These establishments created the platform and context for the invention and mass appeal of cocktails.

Indeed, all who entered Harry Hill's place were greeted with the sign:

Lunches and Juleps
Cobblers and Smashes
To make the tongue waggle
with wit's merry flashes

Once vermouth arrived in New York, it was possible for bartenders* to make "evolved" and "modern" cocktails. It didn't take long for New Yorkers (and eventually all Americans) to take to this startlingly different beverage as both a stand-alone drink and as a cocktail "wonder" ingredient. Despite the Italian producers not exactly having home field advantage—there were a total of 833 Italians in New York City at this time according to the census**—and hardly a Frenchman in site, vermouth quickly made its way onto the cocktail menus of high-society establishments. Delmonico's and the Metropolitan Hotel both carried vermouth on their wine list. It was three dollars a glass at the Metropolitan Hotel (about a week's pay for a typical umbrella seamstress), where the father of mixology (and author of the first-ever cocktail book) Jerry Thomas became head bartender in 1858.[71] And when he published the world's first cocktail book in 1862, he included about twenty recipes for "Hippocras," which were to be drank on their own, much like the "vermouth cocktail" (i.e., just straight vermouth) that would appear just a few years later. The book suggested that this aromatized wine was something to be savored.

---

*   The term "mixologist" was first coined in 1856.

**   The ethnic make-up of New York in the 1860s was overwhelmingly German, Irish, and British, people who preferred to drink Ales, porters, stouts, and, after two Prussian immigrants snuck some bottom-floating yeasts into the country, lagers, which quickly became the drink for certain segments of the population.

Martini & Rossi, (then known as Martini e Sola) shipped its first 100 cases of its sweet vermouth to New York in 1868. Merely five years later, every major vermouth manufacturer from around the world descended on New York to take part in the 1876 United States Centennial Commission International Exhibition. It was a grand affair, filled with agriculture displays, livestock, and vermouth. Lots of it from Europe and South America. Italy dominated the field with fourteen producers including Agosti Brothers, Caretti Brothers, Tarussi, Magnaghi, Rossi, Martini, Sola & Co., Genta, Cavallone, Chicchano, Montini, Galimberti, Isolatelli & Co., and Vittone. The Branca Brothers were also there pouring their vermouth. (There is no mention of Fernet-Branca, the now world famous amaro). Carpano also seems to have missed this event, and they are hardly heard from for the next ninety years, until they begin exporting their "Antica Formula" in 1994. Switzerland sent a producer, and Argentina sent two. France sent only one producer, Dolin Vermouth, which poured its vermouth de Chambery. As best as I can tell, what was poured there had a taste of "pure quinine and pale sherry."[73]

Noilly Prat is not listed as having attended the 1876 Exhibition. There is no record of them being in New York at this time, although they were apparently in New Orleans and San Francisco, and some of the bottles from the 1844 shipment may have been aging nicely in a cellar of one of the fancier Gotham hotels. They did, however, apply for trademark protection, and it was granted on December 18, 1883. The decision was officially announced in New York's *Scientific American* on January 5, 1884, although they did not make it into the *Webster's* dictionary until 1906.[74] The company was handsomely rewarded for its early entrance into the dry vermouth market with a 200-year monopoly in the United States that lasted up until 2008.

To say that dozens of new cocktails were being created in New York concert saloons and hotel bars nightly might be an understatement. Between 1862, when Professor Jerry Thomas published the first ever bartender's manual, and the 1887 reprint, literally thousands of new cocktails had been created.

The most popular (and surviving) cocktail books from the time tell the tale of vermouth's rise from obscurity to the spotlight. *The Flowing Bowl*, compiled by William Schmidt in 1891, lists dozens of vermouth cocktails, most of which call for mostly vermouth with just a dash of liqueur such as Maraschino, absinthe, or fernet. A few years later, George J. Kappeler added to the repertoire with *Modern American Drinks: How to Mix and Serve All Kinds of Cups and Drinks*. Notably, Kappeler included three versions of the Manhattan. A standard, which was made of equal parts whiskey and sweet vermouth, with simple syrup and a cherry; a Dry Manhattan, which left out the simple syrup and the cherry; and the extra dry, which left out the syrup and cherry and substituted Italian vermouth for French.

But vermouth wasn't just used in cocktails; New Yorkers were enjoying it straight or in the popular "vermouth cocktail," which called for vermouth with a dash of Maraschino and a dash of Boker's bitters. Bonfort's *Wine and Liquor* circular promoted a glass of vermouth before dinner as the cultured way to start the meal, and as a "decidedly good thing." By the early 1890s, New Yorkers had begun to commercially produce vermouth and bring it on exhibition. In November 1894, the William H. Hazen Company had incorporated with the intention to sell vermouth cordials. The company had raised $10,000 in capital, and secured William M. Stewart and Edward L. Vaughn of Brooklyn as directors.[75] Emilio Franchi appears to be America's first commercial vermouth producer. He attended the 1893 Exhibit of the State of New York World's Columbian Exposition from May 1 to October 30, 1893. He was also one of three New Yorkers present at the Exhibit. (The other two were a rye producer and Schnapps producer.) By 1914, another New York producer, Amerigo Vespucci, owned by Adolph Votter, filed for a patent for its vermouth. A producer from Cleveland, Ohio, Cordial Panna Company, also obtained a patent for its vermouth.[76] In addition, there were also some very small quantities of American vermouth being produced in California (one company called Rossi P.C.) prior to the turn of the century, but none of these producers appear to have gotten much traction. The imports were of higher quality.

Despite the existence of American vermouth producers in the late nineteenth century, the products were never a significant commercial success. There is no known description of the taste or quality of these products, and so it is unclear whether they failed because they were mostly very bad imitations of their European counterparts, or whether there was something else at play. The American government attempted to help native producers by imposing a discriminatory tax of 35 cents per gallon on foreign vermouths. But it didn't help.

While the American producers struggled, the European producers were making tremendous inroads among bartenders in the 1880s. In the anonymous 1898 book *Cocktails: How to Make Them,* the author explained that "the addition of Vermouth was the first move toward the blending of cocktails." While the original edition of Professor Jerry Thomas's *Bartender Guide* did not list any cocktails containing vermouth, the 1887 reprint lists five recipes calling for vermouth, including the Vermouth Cocktail, the Martinez, and the Manhattan. While his book doesn't specify whether he is using sweet or dry vermouth, given the historical records of what was in New York at this time, we can safely guess that Thomas was using the sweet Italian style. Indeed, the manifold of a ship carrying French liquor in 1884 suggests that very little dry vermouth was in the country at this time. A boat set to dock in July 1884 carried 700 gallons of French alcohol, 243 gallons of gin, and 12 cases (roughly 24 gallons) of vermouth.[77]

By this time, vermouth's popularity in the United States was getting noticed around Europe, and countries beyond France and Italy looked to export their interpretations of the drink to America. At the 1893 New York Exhibit, Spain's Bosch Y Vietti, Buhler & Auge, Mercader Menages, Pi Montello, Pomes, and Viuda de Pablo showed up to pour their Spanish vermouth. The Italian and French producers all appear to have skipped this one.

By the turn of the century, French dry vermouths had infiltrated the country, though to a much smaller degree than the sweet style, and the cocktail books began to categorize drinks by those with sweet vermouths and those with dry. While the Martini and Manhattans that show up in nineteenth-century cocktail books only call for "vermouth," both the Martini and the Manhattan in the popular 1900 cocktail book by George J. Kappeler call for Italian vermouth. This supports the theory that the martinis mentioned in the original cocktail books were referring to sweet Italian vermouth. Harry Johnson's 1900 revision of his 1882 *Bartender's Manual* also just calls for vermouth in his Manhattan and Martini recipe (both equal parts), but he instructs, "It is the bartender's duty to ask the customer whether he desires his drink dry or sweet."[78] Cocktails using vermouth as the primary ingredient became so popular that companies began pre-bottling them. The Heublein Company of Hartford, Connecticut, began marketing club

Early Laws Defining Vermouth

While vermouth was being imported in the late nineteenth century in ever-increasing numbers, there was at that time no American law defining vermouth. Then, and for at least the previous forty years (maybe seventy years), vermouths were being imported into the United States without America having any formal legal definition for what vermouth was. Late-nineteenth-century legal challenges set the stage for how vermouth would come to be defined in the United States.

Dubonnet (which today most anyone would categorize as an aperitif wine and not a vermouth) entered the United States in 1898, as a "medicinal proprietary preparation." Like other French "vermouths" at the time, it was particularly high in quinquina in both constitution and flavor.[79] Although it was being taxed as a tonic (because it was being used as one), the company was also promoting it as a vermouth, and it was being used in cocktails as though it were one. By way of example, in the 1900s one of the most fashionable spring drinks was the Zaza, a cocktail made of gin, Dubonnet, and an orange, served in a cocktail glass. After years of promoting the product differently than what it was being imported as, J. B. Martin, the sole importer of Dubonnet, went before the United States General Appraiser in New York and argued that Dubonnet had "the constituents of vermouth ordinarily dealt with in [America]," and therefore should be taxed as a vermouth, not as a medicine. In other words, because Dubonnet acted like a vermouth, it should be treated as one.

European laws governing the production of vermouth were left to individual countries until the formation of the European Union in the late twentieth century. The legal definitions adopted by European countries have historically been a "mixture of herbs or herb extracts, sugar or grape concentrate, and alcohol." Swiss, Austrian, Italian, French, and German definitions all said practically the same thing throughout the first three quarters of the twentieth century (including that "caramel may be added").

German regulations on vermouth in 1936 required that vermouths had to contain at least 75 percent wine, and not less than 11.9 gm of alcohol per 100 ml, nor more than 14½ gm. Permitted ingredients included hybrid wine, sugar, caramel, citric acid, fining agents, alcohol, herb extracts and milk. In 1919, a report of the Italian Ministry for Industry, which regulates the definition of sweet vermouth wine, particularly with muscat wine from Canelli, highlights the additions of cane sugar, high-proof alcohol, herb extracts, and caramel. The Germans and the Italians got together during the hot summer of 1964, from June 11 to 13, to discuss the minimum standards of vermouth. The main point of these discussions was to ensure that the base wine would account for 75 percent of vermouth, and to come to an agreement on the minimum standards for dry extract, ash, and tartrates.[80]

cocktails. Among the most popular was "The York," consisting of three parts dry vermouth to one part Maraschino (which is just another name for the Vermouth Cocktail).

Given the now undeniable imprint that vermouth was making on the American drinking scene, American vermouth producers realized that they needed to start taking the possibility of domestic production a lot more seriously. As a result, immediately prior to the turn of the twentieth century, Americans got very curious about how the Europeans made their vermouth. A Chicago correspondent for the United States Bureau of Foreign Commerce, acting under Bureau instruction, sent letters to the consular in France and Italy asking for detailed information regarding the preparation of vermouth.[81] The US Consul-General to Paris, John K. Gowdy, received the response one would imagine: he was told, diplomatically speaking, that the Commerce Bureau could go fuck itself, as the recipes are secret. Noting that he has "been unable to secure any reliable information as to the manufacture of vermouth," he went on to say that if the United States were to ask around, he was certain America would obtain a "refusal couched in polite language." Not wanting to be completely non-responsive, he did, however, explain that there were currently three vermouths popular in Paris—Vermouth de Turin, vermouth quina, and vermouth sec. He also offered up in all apparent earnestness that that Vermouth de Turin was manufactured in Turin, vermouth de Milan was manufactured by Fernet, and the most eminent brand of dry "sec" vermouth was Noilly Prat.

Gowdy's colleague John Preston Beecher, US Deputy Consul of Havre, had better luck. He was able to obtain "secret recipes" and wrote back in shocking detail exactly how vermouth is made, and with what. He explained that the manufacturing of vermouth in France was confined almost entirely to the city of Marseilles, where all the important factories existed. Specifically, Havre defined vermouth as "simply an infusion of certain plants and bitter aromatic herbs and roots in a quantity of wine, the degree of which has been strengthened by the addition of one-ninth of its bulk of alcohol."[82] Despite this rather modern definition, the good Consul went on to divulge that the constituents of ordinary French vermouth are dry white wine, muscat wine, wormwood, bitter orange peel, chamomile, water germander, Florentine iris root, centaury, Peruvian

bark, aloes, cinnamon, nutmeg, alcohol at 85 percent, and raspberry juice. And he uncovered and shared the ingredients in ordinary sweet vermouth: sweet white wine, wormwood, helenium, calamus odoratus, centaury, holy thistle, water germander, cinnamon, angelica root, gentian, nutmeg, fresh orange sliced, and alcohol at 85 percent. This dispatch gave exact maceration times (two months), stirred every fifteen days, after which the vermouth should be racked, and then racked again in another two weeks, and explained how to fix vermouth if it starts to cloud up.

Havre also noted that the most commonly used wine was produced in the region of Marseilles and was both abundant and cheap, about 14 cents a gallon. All vermouth exported to the United States at the time was shipped from Marseilles, France, and Turin, Italy. The French shipped $51,586 worth of vermouth to America in 1889. The Italian Consular General was actually just as accommodating. He explained vermouth was understood to be a wine whose "prime material" was the muscat wine of Asti. It was 6 to 11 percent alcohol, 2 to 4 percent sugar, and 2 to 5 percent infusion of aromatic drugs.[83] Again, precise recipes were provided.

The Use of Wormwood in Vermouth

Wormwood is perhaps the bitterest herb known to humankind. For the past several thousand years, when it was included in an aromatized wine, it was used primarily as a medicine. Indeed, notwithstanding some isolated reports of a wormwood wine that was quite palatable, for at least two thousand years, wormwood has been something to suffer through, to take because it was purportedly good for you, not because it was enjoyable. Pliny the Elder, a first-century Roman scholar, wrote that the winner of chariot races was obligated to drink wormwood and wine "to remind him that even glory has its bitter side." During Shakespeare's time it was a common practice among wet nurses to wean babies off of nursing by slathering their nipples with wormwood. Harriet Beecher Stowe starts off her harrowing novel *Uncle Tom's Cabin* with George telling Eliza, "My life is as bitter as wormwood, the very life is burning out of me." Leo Tolstoy in *The Kreutzer Sonata* commented that "another's wife is a white swan, and ours is bitter wormwood." And of course, the coup de grace of how dreadful wormwood tastes: in the *Calvin and Hobbes* comic strip, Calvin's teacher was named "Miss Wormwood."

But let's not beat on wormwood without talking about its virtues, both actual and mythical. Wormwood has enjoyed a long run of being believed to be a panacea for all that ails humankind. Jerome Moses notes that from the earliest times, "Artemisia had special value, especially for women who used them for steam baths." The plants "allegedly could drive sickness from the body, enhance fertility in barren women, break up gall stones, restore the memory, prevent tiredness, and ward off dangerous animals."

Hippocrates, widely acknowledged as the father of modern medicine, prescribed it for menstrual pains, anemia, and rheumatism.[84]

Did Carpano set out to make another wormwood wine when he created vermouth? Was his intention to recreate the ancient Roman drink? I have been unable to uncover any firsthand contemporary evidence of wormwood wine being in sufficient circulation to have actually inspired Carpano. We know that the most popular drink in Germany in the mid-fifteenth century was "Stumwein," "which obtained a faithful following as a social drink." It was made with wine that was infused with numerous botanicals, the principal one being mustard, which is reported to have given a pungent and warming taste. It was eventually banned in Germany in 1472 on account of it being a "bad liquor and prejudicial to health." Significantly, Robert Townsend traveled around Hungary and Vienna in the early 1790s, just a few years after Carpano released his elixir, and he provides a complete description of all the wines he tasted and fails to mention wormwood wine even once.[85]

The ultimate conclusion is that wine infused with a significant amount of wormwood was neither a popular nor widely circulated drink in the mid-1700s, when Carpano would have supposedly been inspired by it. Carpano's Wermut wasn't a wormwood wine; it was the most complex aromatized wine ever created, which played off the name of the most popular Mediterranean plant at the time. This view is consistent with the literature from the time, which always treated the two products as separate. The 1908 publication *Beverages, Past and Present* notes that "the use of wormwood *(Artemisia absinthium)*, in conjunction with wine, making a specie of absinthe, is also common in Transylvania and the adjacent territory. The combination makes a bitter, but nevertheless a most palatable beverage, and when used with discretion is quite wholesome." Vermouth de Torino is listed in a separate section of this publication.

Surprisingly, there does not seem to be any contemporaneous evidence supporting why Carpano called his product "wermut" or vermouth. This lack of knowledge stretches back over a century and a quarter. In 1878, Italian Professor Ottavio Ottavi candidly acknowledged that he was ignorant of "the origin of the drink, which is marketed under the name of vermut or vermouth." He speculated that the name came from Germany, where it is called "Wermouth l'assenzio *(Artemisia absinthium)* e wermuthwein il vino." Twenty-five years later, Arnaldo Strucchi, author of *Il Vermouth di Torino,* acknowledged that he also did not know, and noted only that the name *vermouth,* which is from the German word meaning "wormwood," suggests "that once Germany was preparing a drink made with wormwood, from which vermouth originated, which is a white wine seasoned with a little extract or infusion of drugs and herbs, whose foundation in fact is *Artemisia.*" Not even the Carpano company claims to know why Carpano called his product Wermut. The corporation itself takes the position that "the origin of this name is not certain, but it probably derives from the German word for 'absinthe.'"

Carpano (and all other vermouth producers until the past couple of years) promoted its vermouth as being comprised of the most delicious botanicals from around the world, without mentioning wormwood. Even today, Noilly Prat advertises that its essence comes from aging its wine outside in the elements, and the addition of Roman chamomile and gentian from France, nutmeg from Indonesia, and bitter orange from Tunisia. If a species of *Artemisia* were essential to vermouth's character, one would have expected producers to drop a hint about it somewhere along the road.

And it's not just that these vermouths didn't promote the use of wormwood; they didn't taste of wormwood either. Charles Dickens has described the Turino vermouth served in Paris as reminding him of "the orange peel in syrup in good home-made marmalade."[86] Neither did Martini & Rossi ever promote its use of wormwood until the past few years. When I asked whether Martini vermouth has the slightest flavor of wormwood, their ambassador responded that it is an "under-flavor," meaning it was a flavor that was underneath all the other flavors to support the ones that you can actually taste.

This "under-flavor" position makes sense. Even I can't taste wormwood in traditional European vermouths, and I'm not alone. Since Carpano, the amount of wormwood used in vermouth has steadily decreased to almost nothing. The Italian Professor Ottavi wrote in the first edition of his *Monograph of Luxury Wines and Vinegars* that vermouth was originally mixed with a bit of absinthe, to infuse a special bitter taste, but as of 1878 *Artemisia absinthium* was not the only substance that is infused in wine or alcohol to make vermouth. One century later, Kingsley Amis commented on it in his brill *Everyday Drinking: The Distilled Kingsley Amis,* when he made the offhand comment, "what happened about vermouth, which is *or was* also flavored with wormwood?"[87]

This sentiment continues to the present day, as Martin Doudoroff, the individual behind the website Vermouth101.com, widely regarded as a knowledgeable source on different brands of vermouth, explained to *Imbibe* magazine, "There's so little wormwood in many continental vermouths that, as far as I can tell, it's a formality—it's not like they taste of wormwood in most cases."[88]

BEFORE PROHIBITION

Armed with new capital and new information, Americans set off to start creating quality vermouths. Unfortunately, the American government had changed the tax regulations. The temperance movement was gaining traction, as were the lobbyists of the larger European producers. While Americans had previously had the upper hand from a tax perspective, that too was changing. Domestic vermouth producers were now subject to a quadruple tax on producing vermouth, and as a result vermouth production was hardly financially viable.

In addition to the problems caused by the government, greed and unscrupulous behavior didn't help the American market either. Not everyone was noble and honest. Many American producers began creating "synthetic vermouths," made from alcohol instead of wine.[89] A particularly nasty gentleman was indicted in the Southern District of New York in 1917 on charges of misbranding, a violation of the Food and Drug Act. He was producing vermouth made with less than 50 percent wine and promoting it as having been produced in Italy, which it wasn't. He pleaded guilty and was fined fifty dollars plus costs.[90]

Italian vermouth producers then made an interesting decision. In order to save money from the tax on foreign wines, W.A. Taylor & Co. instituted a lawsuit against the Treasury Department seeking a return of taxes paid pursuant to the War Revenue Act of 1898, which taxed "sparkling or other wine" during the Spanish-American War. The vermouth producers argued that vermouth is not a wine, and therefore should not be subject to the tax. Judge Hough upheld this contention, finding "that the fluid has no other trade name, except vermouth simpliciter, and is, in the minds of American dealers and consumers, an article of its own class, having no more mental relation to wine than chartreuse has to brandy." Accordingly the judge ordered a return of all the taxes paid. While the effects of this legal decision were not immediately felt, the position taken by the producers—that vermouth is not a wine but merely a mixing ingredient—would come back to haunt producers for generations.

Although the number of vermouth cocktails continued to increase (Albert Stevens Crockett noted in the *Old Waldorf-Astoria Bar Book* that over half the

New York City Deputy Commissioner John Leach watches bootlegged liquor being poured out after a raid.

cocktails known prior to World War I had vermouth as an essential ingredient), the quality of spirits improved markedly, and bartenders began tipping their spirits-holding hand a little heavier. By the twentieth century, bartenders had begun to use equal parts spirit and vermouth in their drinks, but the power of vermouth companies was still staggering. Paris, the City of Lights, introduced the world to its first neon sign, three-and-a-half-feet-high glowing white letters in 1913. That sign read Cinzano.[91]

Then, with the advent of refrigeration, drinks got colder and gin began to dominate the cocktail glass. By 1915, cocktails take their pre-Prohibition form of two parts gin (or whiskey) to one part vermouth.[92]

PROHIBITION

The heyday of proper cocktails came to a swift end with the stroke of a pen, beginning on January 17, 1920. After almost a half century of experimentation, with professional bartenders elevating cocktails to a form of high art, the ability to order a balanced, well-mixed cocktail disappeared entirely at the chiming of midnight of a particularly cold night.

While there were over 30,000 bars in New York City during Prohibition (more than double than there were before it), it was a dark time for drinking in general and for vermouth in particular. While bootleggers were able to rip off washbasin gin and put out a decent moonshine, speakeasies didn't hire professional bartenders, and no one was looking for a proper drink while in one. Any intoxicating spirit did just fine. And, of course, if one wanted to bootleg a spirit that would be used solely to intoxicate someone, and not sipped or enjoyed, there would be no need to bootleg vermouth. And indeed, it doesn't appear anyone did. While there are numerous reports of vermouth being confiscated in raids along with other spirits, its use in speakeasies, such as the one on 86 Bedford Street, was not significant. Martini & Rossi tried to maintain some semblance of market participation by sending over a non-alcoholic version of their vermouths. But by the company's own account, the stuff wasn't very good.

THE THIRTIES

Vermouth was welcomed back with open arms as swiftly as any other drink at the end of Prohibition. Indeed, when President Franklin Delano Roosevelt signed the Twenty-First Amendment repealing it, he candidly acknowledged, "What America needs now is a drink." He then poured himself a martini with two parts gin and one part vermouth. Staff writers for *The New Yorker* celebrated the occasion by running out and purchasing a bottle of Noilly Prat. Out of every possible spirit that they could have purchased at the end of a decade of dryness, they chose a bottle of vermouth.

Keen interest in vermouth continued throughout the 1930s. *The New Yorker* magazine dedicated full articles to it every few years that decade, with detailed descriptions of the European brands. Noilly Prat is described simply as "excellent."[93] Martini & Rossi and Cinzano, at the time, still had their vinous quality and had "the unmistakable taste of the Muscat grape."[94] As a result, Americans "went right back to their civilized cocktails of Martinis and Manhattans—cocktails made of vermouth. Why vermouth? Because it fills the true purpose of the cocktail: to stimulate the appetite. It doesn't dull it as sweet drinks do."[95] Numerous European brands began to flood the market with claims that they were *the* vermouth of Europe. Cora in particular made a grand entrance with a heavy advertising budget.[96]

Given the high quality of vermouths and the increasing quality of gins, bartenders largely continued mixing martinis in the classic 2:1 proportion. G. Selmer Fougner, a writer for the *Sun* in 1934, affirmed that the only Martini is two thirds gin and one third vermouth. This proportion appeared to be unflappable. The only problem the European vermouths had during the 1930s, at least according to advertisements put out by Cora Vermouth in *Gourmet* magazine, was that although they were "excellent aperitifs," they were "too sweet for blending purposes for the average American palette."[97] For this reason, *Esquire* magazine suggested making a Martini with a 3:1 gin to vermouth ratio for a "medium martini."[98] Martini & Rossi acknowledged the issue and suggested making the martini with two parts gin to a half part Italian vermouth and a half part dry vermouth.

Even with these now decreasing ratios of vermouth, the import numbers were astronomical. Vermouth was the largest selling "wine" in the country, outselling table wine by a mile. And it was without a doubt the most popular because of its perceived elegance and sophistication. In 1937, one million gallons of wine were used to produce vermouth. To put this in perspective, at the time's dominant ratio of 2:1 gin to vermouth, this is enough vermouth for 128 million Martinis and Manhattans. (In 1935 there were only 127 million people in America, with over a quarter of the population under eighteen). Of course, all of this vermouth came from overseas producers.

The quality of American vermouth immediately after Prohibition was poor. This is understandable, as Americans, obviously, had not been permitted to produce vermouth for the previous thirteen years, and so no one was doing it. Moreover, prior to 1936 there was a quadruple tax on producing vermouth in America, as opposed to the single tax imposed on foreign producers. American wineries took their concerns to their local politicians and began to make a racket. And it worked. The federal government started to take notice of the potential size of the vermouth market, and it made the move to put American producers on equal footing. In 1940 the laws were changed again to completely equalize the taxes imposed on foreign and domestic vermouths. This change resulted in a seismic shift in American's ability to produce quality vermouth. As of 1941, American vermouth was the fastest growing item in the United States wine trade.[99]

WORLD WAR II

In the next year, of course, came the hostilities overseas. All quality vermouths immediately prior to the Second World War were imports from Italy and France, and with those two countries tied up in conflict, both countries' producers struggled to keep up with demand. Martini & Rossi began shipping their products from Spain and Argentina. But anti-Italian and anti-French sentiment gave Americans a strong justification for eliminating their most cherished products from their homes and bars. As a result, the flow of imported vermouth from Europe "slowed down as gradually as an automobile which has smashed into a telephone pole."[100]

> *"A quality vermouth product is produced only by the cellarman who lives with the product and whose life and professional pride is tied with it."*
>
> —Otto F. Jacoby

American producers were more than happy to step in and begin an appropriate campaign of reminding Americans that, to paraphrase Ginger Rogers to Fred Astaire, anything you can do, I can do backwards. Americans struggled to produce even fair vermouth immediately after Prohibition. During the war years, however, when they were the only game in town, they began hiring experts from overseas and investing significant sums in research and development. This put the American work ethic to the test. The war cut supplies by nine-tenths. The Roma Wine Company in California was quick to realize what the trouble overseas was doing to the European producer's ability to reliably deliver the 1.6 million gallons of vermouth Americans needed to quench their thirst for Martinis, Manhattans, Vermouth Cocktails, and Highballs.

Otto F. Jacoby of the Berkeley Yeast Laboratory sounded the battle horn in 1948, when he published an article in *Wines and Vines* lamenting the desire of vermouth producers to merely mimic the Italian and French styles, and the lack of any true American vermouths. "It would be much more to the point," Jacoby argued "to have the objective of producing a strictly American or Californian Type Vermouth."[101] Jacoby obviously didn't write this at the start of his endeavors, as the Berkeley Yeast Laboratory had already put together an impressive catalogue of 225 bottles, each with a different herb or other botanical extract. Jacoby was also the first American to suggest moving beyond the "traditional" fifty or so known herbs and seasonings that could be discerned by reading the various published formulas. According to Jacoby, American producers needed to experiment with "every non-poisonous plant with a pronounced taste or odor"[102] and could potentially produce an excellent vermouth. Rather than keep all of his learning to himself, he essentially published an expert's guide for producing vermouth. In his 1948 article, Jacoby did something no American appears to have done before: he publicly disclosed the secrets of vermouth production including how to develop the formula, how to balance the formula, and how to manufacture it.

After this, American vermouth production swelled, in both quality and quantity. The United States had two principal vermouth producing sections. California had over 70 vermouth-producing wineries,[103] and New York had over 116 vermouth-production centers. New York and California accounted for over 94 percent of all vermouth produced in the United States.

Advertising for the burgeoning industry played to American patriotism. New York producer Gambarelli & Davitto put together a full frontal assault on the European producers by running ads that paid homage to highlights of American history, and to what they called "native wine," presumably a precursor to American vermouth. One ad suggested that the Boston Tea Party should have been called the Boston Vermouth Party, because colonists preferred American wine to imported tea.[104] Another noted that in 1609, on the shores of the lake that now bears his name, the bold French Explorer Samuel de Champlain raised aloft a glass of native wine, possibly a predecessor of Gambarelli & Davitto American vermouth.[105] Vermouth consumption reached three million gallons by 1943, a 40 percent increase since 1935. By 1944, that number more than doubled.[106] (Americans tend to drink during wartime and immediately afterward. Since our country averages a major war every twenty years, we're always drinking.)[107] Despite all of these advertisements and the existence of smaller vermouth companies, American wineries eventually took a commanding market share of the domestic vermouth market. Gallo, United Vintners, and Mogen David (owners of G&D vermouth) had captured 15.4 percent, 14.4 percent, and 10.2 percent of the market, respectively. Vermouth Industries of America moved its production plant to midtown Manhattan, where it remained the country's largest vermouth production center for decades.

THE *MAD MEN* YEARS

Something began to happen to the American psyche following WWII. While it was a time of unprecedented growth, anyone who has seen an episode of *Mad Men* knows that the great flight to the suburbs shattered us in many ways. Americans started acting differently after the war. They started drinking more often and larger amounts. They wanted drinks that would drown their sorrows. This resulted in "violent protest of this wishy-washy type of cocktail" (cocktails made with half or even one-third vermouth), and drinkers began demanding that their Martinis be made by adding a drop of vermouth to the cocktail glass, swirling it around, and emptying any remaining vermouth before filling up the glass with 100 percent gin.[108]

As men returned from the war and found women in increasingly powerful roles, a faux-masculinity appeared, which resulted in men demanding "stronger" drinks. American historian Bernard DeVoto summed up the feeling of the age in his 1948 book, *The Hour: A Cocktail Manifesto*: "Whiskey and vermouth cannot meet as friends and the Manhattan is an offense against piety. With dry vermouth it is disreputable, with sweet vermouth it is disgusting. It signifies that the drinker, if male, has no spiritual dignity and would really prefer white mule; if female, a banana split."[109] Writing for *The New Yorker* around this time, E. B. White commented on this turning of the tide in the postwar years. In a Talk of the Town column, he wrote, "The most noticeable changes in New York are the increasing dryness of its Martinis and the increasing irritability of its hackmen [taxi drivers]." White noted, dryly, that "only the most delicate chemical test would reveal traces of vermouth in the Martinis that the bartenders are stirring up these days."[110]

Perhaps the most telling turn of the tide came on July 25, 1955,[111] at the twenty-third National Housewares Show in Atlantic City, where U.S. manufacturers presented to the American public all of the inventions and gadgets that would soon be hitting stores shelves. The only comparative event today would be the announcement of the next iPhone. What was presented then seems silly now, but imagine the world in 1950, when most U.S. citizens did not own a toaster oven or a vacuum cleaner and you can get a sense of what these shows were like. In 1955, our country's best and brightest put on display an alarm clock that turned on and off with the touch of a finger, a rug cleaner that was safe to drink, and an atomizer for spraying the merest dash of vermouth into your martinis. Even high-end jewelry producers catered to their clientele's desire to show off how little vermouth they put into their Martinis. Tiffany's, the glamorous jewelry dealer, produced a tiny silver oilcan meant to be used in dispensing vermouth.[112]

The 1950s' march toward modernity brought about not just newfound names for the Martini—such as the fashionable Montgomery Martini made at a 15:1 gin-heavy ratio, and named after a British field marshal who never went into battle unless those were the odds in his favor—but also premixed cocktails. Heublein cocktail mixers began selling premixed Martinis and Manhattans. At a time when premade TV dinners were all the rage, so too did consumers want their drinks premade for them. It was "the modern way."[113] Keeping in line with the times, these premixed cocktails were promoted as being "mostly gin" and "strictly for the lion hearted."[114] Even the IRS changed the tax rules to bring them more in line with contemporary tastes; in 1954 tax laws were changed to permit premixed and bottled Martini cocktails to be mixed 5:1, as opposed to the prior 3:1 requirements. Vermouth was getting pushed to the side.

Americans were clearly moving toward stiffer drinks. And as they did, the media ran various stories about the social ills of alcohol. After Prohibition failed, alcoholism moved from being considered a moral/social failing to a treatable illness. Charles Jackson's somber 1944 novel *The Lost Weekend* brought unprecedented attention to alcohol and alcoholism. *LIFE* magazine ran a huge expose on liquor, which combined studies in medicine and psychiatry to "bring enlightenment to the 30,000 year old problem of drinking."[115]

The response of the European manufacturers to the media outcry against alcohol was to misunderstand what the people actually wanted. Perhaps they paid too much attention to all the negative publicity, but whatever the reason, the European producers doomed themselves to irrelevance by blindly following what they believed was public consensus. Martini & Rossi began running advertisements highlighting how vermouth was the equivalent of "moderation," suggesting that people (particularly women) did not have to miss the fun by abstaining.[116]

As a result, there was a significant shift in how vermouth producers advertised their products in the late 1950s. Advertising budgets ballooned, and a no-expense-spared war erupted between the major producers. Noilly Prat hired the dandy comic artist Peter Arno, who drew advertisements for them when he wasn't out on the town with a starlet.[117] Martini & Rossi hired the best and brightest advertisers one could hire, and their posters remain a sign of elegance and hipness decades later. But more importantly, vermouth producers all but abandoned the notion that vermouth could be drunk straight and began to advertise their vermouths as the go-to vermouths for *mixing* in cocktails, acknowledging that using smaller amounts of vermouth was perfectly appropriate.

There began a race to the bottom and an ever-increasing shift toward less differentiated vermouths. Foreign producers began to reformulate their vermouths made for export to the United States into lighter, less flavorful styles. Whereas for all of its history, vermouths were produced as aperitifs meant to be sipped on their own, in the late 1950s European producers stopped using the quality wines traditionally called for, and began advertising that their vermouths were "not aperitifs" but were "made for mixing."[118] Gancia Vermouth was among the first Italian producers to explicitly trumpet its product as a mixer for martinis.[119] Even Martini & Rossi began advertising its vermouths as "a flavoring agent."[120] Like a sheep led to slaughter, Cinzano went right along with this position. Reasoning, if you can believe it, that it was more profitable if customers order a 5:1 martini over a 3:1 martini, because, if given the former, the customer is more likely to order another one.

With this huge expenditure on advertising, the major European producers began to change their formulas, including their base wines, for the vermouths being shipped to America. In addition to switching the wine base, some European producers began to move their production facilities to neighboring countries, so as to appear more "authentic." Cinzano introduced its dry vermouth, which, although the company had been in Italy for the past 150 years, was being imported from France. Noilly Prat, which dominated the French vermouth market for the past century and a half, was now exporting its sweet vermouth from Italy. And it changed its formula to reflect America's changing tastes, knocking down the sweetness of its "less sweet, sweet vermouth" to respond to Manhattan lovers who were forced to consistently say, "a little less sweet, if you please."[121]

Gancia Vermouth struck particularly hard at the notion of vermouth being a stand-alone aperitif or a beverage with sufficient character to lend anything to a cocktail other than a reduction in alcohol content. They asserted that "aperitif vermouth should never be used in a cocktail." Americans, the company insisted, were making cocktails the wrong way. They should be using vermouth that is designed specifically for mixing, as opposed to the traditional European vermouths that were made to be drunk straight. Gancia insisted that its vermouth was "never to be drunk straight."[122] Cora, in an advertising series that would not have made it past a junior level associate in today's world, promoted itself by explaining that "a good vermouth should mind its own business," with a photograph of a woman holding her finger against her lips to shush herself. Cora noted that "no man wants to be told how to make a martini. And certainly no vermouth should interfere with his taste or his craftsmanship." Cora was "the Quiet Vermouth."[123]

As a result, by 1958 the differentiation of the notable mainstream brands was so narrow that no one, connoisseur or not, could tell the difference between any of the vermouth brands.

Nor was the response of American vermouth producers any better. Producers began taking horrifying shortcuts to make the cheapest, barely palatable vermouth possible. After leaving his post in the U.S. Internal Revenue Service, Peter Valaer disclosed some of the findings he had made while working as a clerk there. Valaer occupied the envious position of having access to the formula of every vermouth producer who sought approval for his or her product with the U.S. Treasury Department. In conducting this analysis he found that many American vermouth producers used "odds and ends" and "defective wines that were high in volatile acidity," i.e., vinegar. He also disclosed that many of the American dry vermouths contained fewer than ten botanicals, and that many producers used the same exact recipe for the sweet and dry styles, but they used a smaller ratio of botanicals for the dry, and obviously no caramel.[124]

American producers also played to the notion that vermouth was subservient to spirits. Lejon Vermouth, produced in California, touted itself as a vermouth that "knows its place in a martini." So subtle, Lejon prided and preened, it makes a "3:1 taste like a 5:1."[125] The campaign for Cresta, another American brand, exclaimed "At last … a White Vermouth created especially for the Dry Martini."[126] It criticized the "pronounced golden color and strong herbal flavor" of traditional dry vermouths, "both American and foreign." Tribuno vermouth, another product blended for American tastes, boasted that it "never overpowers."

These practices by global producers did not go unnoticed. Post-WWII reports criticize the ever-increasing frequency of production concerns such as watering down of the wine and using artificial flavor extracts.[127]

The San Francisco Wine Institute noticed what was happening by the mid-1960s. Reviewing the old literature, which described the delicious flavors of the Muscat grape, it criticized this new use of "cheap, young neutral-flavored wines" that were now being used as a base for vermouth in Europe. Many Americans began lamenting this departure from the distinct, quality wines that had been used around the turn of the century.

While both American and European vermouth producers were creating cheaper vermouths with less and less flavor and soul, a large subset of the American population was feeling increasingly modern, and was looking for new ways to drink. Once again, the federal government played its hand. Federal regulations changed to permit the production of "special natural wines." In other words, wines to which various flavors could be added. Prior to this amendment, the only permissible "flavored wine" in the United States was vermouth. Now, however, California wineries had the ability to just add single flavors to their wines without paying any additional rectification taxes.

Many of you will remember how this story goes. Gallo released Thunderbird in 1957. Shortly thereafter, the Code of Federal Regulations was changed again, this time to permit the carbonation of wine (but not fortification). And so the early seeds were planted that would eventually permit the creation of Boone's Farm.

While Thunderbird and Boone's Farm today rank lower on the totem pole than the damp earth, at the time these were fresh, modern, and futuristic drinks. After all, it's not every day that the head of the United Vintners tells the members of the Los Angeles advertising club that they are "wasting [their] time talking about port, sherry, muscatel, burgundy & sauterne because such wines belonged to the past: the future lay with new wines [i.e., flavored and carbonated]."[128] This was in 1962.

THE HIPPIE GENERATION

"Vermouth sales will double over the next decade."

—John L. Tribuno, **1965**

"Young people do not like Martinis and they're not drinking them. Ever! Anywhere!"

—James Villas in *Esquire*, **1973**

The Martini. The Manhattan. Cocktail Hour. Vermouth. These things stood for everything phony to the Baby Boomer generation. They stood for the bourgeois values and social snobbery that the Hippie movement rejected. They also, as so many of these kids witnessed, resulted in jaded alcoholism, latent masochism, and broken families. As the Greatest Generation started turning their martinis into simple glasses of gin, the kids took notice. John Cheever captured this sentiment in "The Country Husband," "The Sorrows of Gin," and "The Swimmer"—all stories about dysfunctional families ripped apart by loneliness and alcoholism. But most of these kids didn't need to read Cheever to understand how alcohol was destroying their families. Having lived through the downside of this ceremonial drinking of Martinis, the idea of ending the working day with a stiff drink was sworn off by the new generation.

In 1967, for the first time in history, table wine sales exceeded fortified wine sales. The decline would take off sharply from here. By 1978, the majority of Americans who bought vermouth were over forty-five years old, and the overwhelming majority of those were women.[129] Hardly anyone under the age of thirty-five ever bought a bottle of vermouth.

And so it was for the next thirty years.

European Union Legal Definition of Vermouth

The legal requirements regarding vermouth production in Europe were eventually consolidated after the formation of the European Union. EU law defines vermouth as an "aromatized wine," "whose characteristic taste has been obtained by the use of appropriate substances of *Artemisia* species."

Artemisia is a broad, diverse genus of plants, which includes over 400 different sub-species belonging to the daisy family, Asteraceae. *Artemisia* includes hundreds of species, among them sagebrush, mugwort, sagewort, wormwood, tarragon, and southernwood. An earlier, unpublished draft of the law provided that vermouth must contain "Wormwood *(Artemisia vulgaris)*." This draft was changed to only require any species of *Artemisia* before being passed in 1991.

CLASSIC
COCKTAILS

ROCKS   COCKTAIL

INGREDIENTS

2 oz. dry vermouth

1 oz. Greenhook Ginsmith gin

1 thinly sliced lemon peel

INSTRUCTIONS

To build, pour the ingredients into a mixing glass with ice, stir 40-50 times until cold, but before ice crystals form. Strain into a rocks glass or a cocktail glass.

SUGGESTED VERMOUTHS

Atsby Amberthorn

Ransom Dry

Uncouth Dry Hopped or Wildflower

Vya Dry

MARTINI

Enough books have been written about the Martini to fill the Grand Canyon, and so putting together a short pithy header is a little like having Georgia O'Keeffe asking you to paint a flower. There is this immediate and irrepressible thought that it's all been said before. But here goes.

I call this cocktail the Martini Reviver, even though it is actually the recipe for the original Martini (called the Turf Cocktail) in the 1884 *Bar Keeper's Handbook*, because I believe this recipe revives the original drink to a sublime experience. This is how the drink was originally intended. Full bodied, floral, colorful amber!

ROCKS

INGREDIENTS

2 oz. Atsby Armadillo Cake Vermouth

1 oz. Hudson Rye

1 dash bitters (Adam Elmegirab's Boker's works well)

1 fresh bing cherry

INSTRUCTIONS

To build, pour the ingredients into a mixing glass with ice, stir 40 times. A Manhattan should always be served chilled up, in a rocks glass. Garnish with a single cherry.

VARIATIONS

Substitute the whiskey for another spirit for intriguing variations: Anejo Manhattan (with Anejo tequila), Rum Manhattan (with dark rum).

MANHATTAN

There is little debate that the Manhattan Cocktail was first served in a bar in downtown Manhattan, by a man named "Black" who owned a shop on Broadway "ten paces South of Houston in the 1860s."[72] Just what was happening ten paces south of Houston? According to a post published in the *New York Clipper* on February 20, 1864, "The block on Broadway between Prince and Houston Streets is just about the liveliest part of New York City, both in and out of doors. Showmen, actors, pugilists, and fast men of every description are all attracted to this spot by some sort of magnetic influence. And we might say that night is turned into day; for by the time most of the saloons get closed, the milkman, butcher, country marketer, and gutter snipe are just commencing their day's business." In Manhattan one hundred and fifty years later, this cocktail remains the one of choice for turning night into day.

COUPE

INGREDIENTS

1½ oz. Atsby Armadillo Cake
Vermouth

1½ oz. Whistle Pig Rye

1 bar spoon of Tempus Fugit
Gran Classico or Campari

1 large sliced orange peel

INSTRUCTIONS

Build the cocktail by pouring
the individual ingredients into
a mixing glass filled with ice.
Stir 40-50 times, and strain
into a 3 oz. cocktail coupe.
Garnish with a twist of orange.
Start reading Henry Miller's
Quiet Days in Clichy.

BOULEVARDIER

Harry McElhone is credited with this beauty,
even though we know from the postscript of
his 1927 *Barflies and Cocktails* that it was the
American dandy and exile Erskine Gwynne
who "crashed the party" with it several years
earlier. Gwynne's literary magazine *The
Boulevardier* was a bit of a cause célèbre in
Paris, where Harry was tending bar in the
1920s, and Gwynne had the foresight to take
out a full-page ad at the back of *Barflies* to
promote it, further solidifying the relationship
between literature and cocktails. Gwynne was
as good with a mixing glass as he was with fiction. He wasn't your run-of-the-mill wealthy
socialite; he was one who had the good sense
to publish the early transcendent works of
Joyce, Hemingway, Dos Passos, and others.

While it might seem obvious that perking
up a Manhattan with some extra bitters from
Campari would improve (or rather, change)
an already perfect drink, Gwynne was the
first one to execute it—that night it was for
a group of young French girls at the end of
typical Parisian evening. And the world is all
the better for it.

TUMBLER

INGREDIENTS

2 oz. sweet vermouth

½ oz. London dry gin

½ oz. bitter orange liqueur

1 large orange peel

INSTRUCTIONS

Pour all three ingredients into a tumbler glass filled with ice and stir 3 times. Garnish with a large orange peel.

SUGGESTED VERMOUTHS

Atsby Armadillo Cake

Carpano Antica Formula

Uncouth Beet Eucalyptus

VARIATION

Swipe out the gin for soda water and you have an Americano.

NEGRONI

While not nearly as old as the Manhattan or Martini, the Negroni has earned the title of classic cocktail, notwithstanding the original rather bland description of how it was invented: i.e., that the Count Camillo Negroni asked a bartender in 1919 Florence to make him something stronger than his go-to aperitif, the Americano. The Negroni is not so much a specific cocktail as a suggested ratio for spirit, vermouth, and liqueur, 1:1:1. This ratio tends to work with the standard sweet vermouths, but doesn't work as well with the less sweet, more flavorful American vermouths coming onto the market.

This recipe breaks from the traditional 1:1:1 ratio, and while some may scream blasphemy, I'm willing to bet that the overwhelming majority of you will thank me for it. My problem with the traditional Negroni ratio is that the Campari runs roughshod over the other ingredients. If you're using a cheaper vermouth, which is mostly contributing sweetness, then this version is okay, but to elevate the cocktail to the sublime, lower the Campari and up the vermouth, the result is a much more interesting, complex, and enjoyable drink.

ROCKS

INGREDIENTS

1½ oz. sweet vermouth

1½ oz. Scotch

1 dash celery bitters

1 thinly sliced celery stalk

INSTRUCTIONS

Build the cocktail by pouring the vermouth and scotch into a rocks glass and then adding 2 dashes of celery bitters. Swirl mixture in the glass without ice, and garnish with a thinly sliced celery stalk that has been soaked in the vermouth.

SUGGESTED VERMOUTHS

Hammer & Tongs

Ransom Sweet

Vya Sweet

ROB ROY

Everyone has an immediate, visceral reaction when they hear "Robinson Crusoe"—thoughts of adventure, overcoming fear, personal growth, isolation, loneliness, fear of death, and (of course) confronting cannibals while surviving as a castaway. For this we can thank English author Daniel Defoe, who pretty much invented modern fiction in 1719 with the book of this name. Another of his heroes survives today, not in human form but in cocktail. Rob Roy MacGregor, a hero and nationalist (if you're Scottish) or a traitor, cattle thief, and general villain (if you're English), was romanticized in Defoe's 1723 pamphlet *Highland Rogue* (written while Rob Roy was still alive). William Wordsworth did his part by writing the poem "Rob Roy's Grave" in 1803, which described Roy as a Scottish Robin Hood, and the tale continued to grow through portrayals in novels and plays throughout the century. By 1894, the story had reached Broadway, and the surrounding bars did their part to honor the man and the myth by creating a cocktail with Roy's hometown distillate, Scotch. The Rob Roy is basically a Manhattan with Scotch, but if made with the right ingredients it can leave you with all the positive thoughts left behind by all of Defoe's characters.

BOBBY BURNS

What's the difference between a Rob Roy and a Bobby Burns you ask? This may sound like the start of a joke, but it's a legitimate question, and the answer is (1) Robert Burns was a Scottish poet who may or may not have anything to do with the name of this cocktail, and (2) the addition of an herb-infused liqueur (either Benedictine or Drambuie). Drambuie, of course, is a distant relative of vermouth, sharing the common ingredients of honey, herbs, and spices; the only difference is that the base is malt whisky. Benedictine is similar and made from a recipe that includes twenty-seven herbs and spices. So it's not surprising that a mixologist would think to combine these liqueurs with vermouth, and many such bartenders did. Some of the most esteemed cocktail bars, including the Savoy and the Waldorf Astoria, featured the drink. When mixed in these perfect proportions, the cocktail is legendary.

ROCKS

INGREDIENTS

1½ oz. sweet vermouth

1½ oz. Scotch

¼ oz. Benedictine or Drambuie

1 pinch of saffron

INSTRUCTIONS

Pour all ingredients into a rocks glass and stir several times. Garnish with a pinch of saffron.

SUGGESTED VERMOUTHS

Atsby Armadillo Cake

Hammer & Tongs Sac'Résine or L'Afrique

COCKTAIL

INGREDIENTS

1½ oz. sweet vermouth

1½ oz. London dry gin

1 dash Maraschino liqueur

1 dash lemon bitters

INSTRUCTIONS

Pour all ingredients into a mixing glass. Stir 40 times, pour into a coupe or martini glass, which has been sprayed with Pernod. No garnish.

SUGGESTED VERMOUTHS

Atsby Armadillo Cake

Dolin Rouge

Uncouth Serrano Chile Lavender

MARTINEZ

This is a true classic cocktail, predating the Martini by five years and much more reflective of the drinking styles of the 1880s. This drink eventually fell out of fashion because the combination of Old Tom gin and sweet vermouth was found to be too cloying even for the sweet-tooths of the late nineteenth century. This modernized version swaps out the Old Tom for London dry gin and suggests "sweet vermouths" that are less viscous than the standard sweet vermouths.

COCKTAIL MAKING HINT

The colder a drink, the less sweet it will seem to taste. So adjust how many mixes you give based on the ingredients of your cocktail. With a drink like the Martinez, which calls for a sweet vermouth and Maraschino liqueur, it is important to make sure that it is very cold; otherwise the Maraschino can start to overpower.

FORD COCKTAIL

COUPE

This cocktail makes its first appearance in George Kappeler's *Modern American Drinks: How to Mix and Serve All Kinds of Cups and Drinks* in 1900, and is essentially a Bobby Burns where you swap out the Scotch for Old Tom gin, and sweet vermouth for a drier style. The secret to this cocktail is to use a very flavorful dry vermouth.

INGREDIENTS

1½ oz. dry vermouth

1½ oz. Old Tom gin

1 tbsp. Benedictine

1 dash orange bitters

Orange peel

INSTRUCTIONS

Pour all ingredients into a mixing glass and stir 25 to 30 times. Strain into a coupe glass. Garnish with a twist of an orange peel.

SUGGESTED VERMOUTHS

Atsby Amberthorn

Noilly Prat Ambre

Regal Rogue Dry

Uncouth Dry Hopped

FORGOTTEN COCKTAILS

ROCKS

BROOKLYN COCKTAIL

INGREDIENTS

2 oz. Uncouth Vermouth

1 oz. rye

¼ oz. of Amer Picon
(or other amaro)

1 bing cherry

INSTRUCTIONS

Pour the ingredients into a
rocks glass without ice, and stir
with a mixing spoon. Garnish
with a fresh bing cherry.

The Brooklyn Cocktail is a dry Manhattan
that has been improved by the judicious use of
amaro. The original recipe called for a dash
of Maraschino liqueur as well, but it's frankly
not necessary and only creates a consistency
that is more syrupy and viscous than what
people can tolerate today, though it was more
popular when the drink was created. In the
same way I believe a true Manhattan should
be made with a vermouth from Manhattan, a
true Brooklyn cocktail should use a vermouth
from Brooklyn.

METROPOLE COCKTAIL AND METROPOLITAN COCKTAIL

The Metropole and Metropolitan Cocktails are basically a dry Manhattan and Manhattan with apple brandy instead of whiskey. It's not clear why these cocktails never made a bigger splash than they did, other than the obvious argument that whiskey was of a higher quality than the brandy being distilled in the late 1800s. Today, however, there are so many phenomenal apple brandies on the market, as well as really high quality Calvados, that this is a cocktail that can go toe to toe with the Manhattan. I expect this cocktail to make a comeback.

ROCKS

INGREDIENTS

2 oz. vermouth (sweet or dry)

1 oz. apple brandy or Calvados (always use an 80 proof brandy)

1 apple slice

INSTRUCTIONS

Pour all ingredients into a mixing glass with ice and stir 10 times. Strain into a rocks glass, and garnish with an apple slice.

chapter three

AMERICAN VERMOUTH TODAY

The early years of the twenty-first century have been an unprecedented time in vermouth production, both in the United States and throughout the world. In 2009 there were no modern American vermouth producers. In 2012 there were three. Now there are dozens of companies commercially producing vermouth in the United States, with dozens more working to perfect their formulas as I write. Regardless of its volatile popularity, it is particularly fascinating that for the past 200 years vermouth has been produced essentially the same way, resulting in vermouths with minimal flavor differences other than the split between dry and sweet. Today however, American producers are making vermouths that taste nothing like one another, and nothing like their European counterparts.

DRY
Wormwood
Vya
VERMOUTH
APERITIF
Sweet
PREMIUM CALIFORNIA
WINES INFUSED WITH
SELECTED BOTANICALS
BOTTLE
07466

VYA VERMOUTH

SAN JOAQUIN VALLEY, CALIFORNIA

When the twelve-foot, 11,875-pound Waterford Crystal New Year's Eve ball dropped in Times Square at midnight to kick off 1999, it was reflecting more than sixteen million vibrant hues and tints and billions of patterns that shone out in a dizzying kaleidoscope of color. Americans were partying in the streets across the country, just as the artist formerly known as Prince said they would. Times were good. Computer programmers still had a full 365 days to work out the final kinks before Y2K, the Dot-com bubble was large and unpopped, Bill Clinton was in office, and *Sex and the City* had just aired its second season. Americans were ordering Cosmopolitans and Appletinis.

The thought of drinking a proper cocktail with copious amounts of vermouth—or any for that matter—was on very few, if any, minds. European producers continued to ship over their low-quality, made-for-export versions of vermouth in depressing and ever decreasing numbers. The last respectable American vermouth producer had shuttered its doors decades before. There were, of course, several brands like Tribuno and Spatola that were still being offered for sale under the "vermouth" label, though always on the lowest shelf in the dustiest corner of the liquor store. And for good reason. The producers who were manufacturing decent vermouths during the 1940s and '50s had all fallen to the anti-cocktail craze of the late twentieth century.

On the other side of the country, one old Napa Valley winemaker, Andrew Quady, was finishing up a light dinner when a friend rather fortuitously made an off-hand comment about how much vermouth sucked. Quady agreed for the most part, but noted that the vermouth being sold in America was different than what was being sold in Europe. To prove the point, Quady created Vya Vermouth and the following year became America's first quality vermouth producer in several generations.

Quady knew a little about vermouth and its history in the California wine industry. He had studied winemaking at one of America's most prestigious oenological schools, the University of California at Davis. He was fortunate enough to have taken a class with Maynard Andrew Amerine, the visionary, pioneering wine researcher widely recognized for developing California's wine industry.

Amerine was no slouch, and his effect on America's drinking culture continues to today. He is largely responsible for creating not just our wine industry, but arguably the current craft vermouth movement as well. His books on the subject gave inspiration to generations of growers, producers, and even chefs. Amerine set the foundation for other giants such as Harold McGee and Alton Brown to build upon his work. Without him, the Judgment of Paris, where a panel of world renowned French judges took part in a blind taste test comparing French to Californian wines (and picked the Californian) likely would have turned out differently than it did. Amerine and another professor, A. J. Winkler, spent the better part of the late 1930s studying various grape varieties to determine which grew best in California, where, and under what conditions. Amerine studied more than 3,000 wine samples, a task that required him to taste twenty wines every morning before lunch and twenty wines after for a whole decade. He ultimately figured out that California had five completely unique climate regions, and that different grape varieties would do better in some regions than others. The influence of the pair's conclusions, published in a 1944 article in *Hilgardia,* a popular agricultural research magazine, cannot be overstated. Growers and producers followed his advice, and the quality of California wine increased exponentially.

The breadth of Amerine's interest in wine went beyond table wines. He also understood how important vermouth production was to the American wine industry, and in December 1974 he published *Vermouth: An Annotated Bibliography,* listing in A-to-Z format an abstract of every book and article ever published about vermouth. The same year, he also dedicated one class that semester to the production of vermouth. Quady was in that class. At the time of that lecture, there was nothing as hopelessly square as vermouth—nothing as sad and preposterous. No hip winemaker wanted to touch it with a ten-foot pole. Everyone in the class was inspired by the recent interest in top-quality table wines and secretly vowed to never go back to making such an ancient libation. Even Quady admits he walked out of that class never imagining he'd ever look at those notes again. But he did keep them . . . in a trunk in his garage.

Twenty-five years later, directly following the dinner where his friend questioned the possibility of ever making a decent vermouth, Quady went back to his fading notes and tried to remember what Amerine had said during that lecture. Quady decided to make a quality vermouth that was imitative of the European styles but had a California distinction. Quady had the good fortune of living in San Joaquin Valley, a region that—while quiet and unassuming—had the right soil and temperature to grow Orange Muscat grapes, which provide a nice viscosity for vermouth and were used in the Piedmont region of Italy where vermouth was first commercialized.

Quady settled on a mix of Muscat and Colombard grapes for color and added flavor. During conferences and in discussions, Quady told the story of how after settling on a wine, he rented a donkey and rode it high into the Sierra Mountains looking for edible plants to use in his vermouth. While there is some poetry in that story, he also acknowledges that he sources botanicals from around the world—lavender, galangal root, orris root, angelica, linden, alfalfa, and various mints. He then fortified his vermouths with a neutral grape brandy, naming them Sweet and Extra Dry.

Quady's vermouths are very close to the traditional European styles. The sweet is a little spicier than the sweet European vermouths and not quite as bitter, while the dry is significantly more herbal than traditional dry. With Amerine's notes as their premise, his blends are closer to the historical vermouths produced in America that were developed during the War years. For this reason I don't place Vya squarely in the same category as the other American craft vermouths, but Quady's contribution cannot be denied, and he is singularly responsible for carrying the torch that lit up where we are today.

But what about the name? The Broadway playwright and producer Zack Manna is probably one of the best storytellers to recount the myth of the product's name: Quady had finally figured out his recipe for both his vermouths and believed they were ready for tasting. He started by giving some to a small group of his friends without telling them what they were drinking. The first friend to try the Sweet asked what he was drinking, and when Quady disclosed that it was vermouth, the friend replied "Vermouth your ass. This tastes too good to be vermouth." As a result, Quady decided to name his vermouth Vya.

While a great story, particularly when Manna tells it three vodka Martinis in, it turns out not to be true. In fact, there is no story behind the name, other than that it has a *V* in it, which was intended for people to associate with vermouth. However, at the time associating anything with vermouth seemed to be a bad idea. After the vermouths were released, Quady's distributor in New York City found it difficult to convince liquor storeowners and bar managers to even taste them, let alone buy them. Quady's hope that Vya would be embraced as an aperitif did not quite pan out. In an attempt to figure out how to get industry professionals to sample the product, Quady's NYC sales rep decided he had to stop using the word "vermouth" and so began asking potential purchasers if they would like to try his "Vya." Even this, however, failed to convince people to taste it. Finally, when the rep was asked by a spirits buyer at a wine and liquor store, "what is Vya?" the rep simply replied, "It's Vermouth, You Asshole."

Vya never created any excitement about the category. While the brand found some devotees around the country and had decent sales domestically and abroad, it languished—a novelty in a dead and forgotten category—for the next decade.[*]

OH MY, OH MY

2 oz. Vya Sweet
1 oz. Vya Extra Dry
¾ oz. Essensia
1 dash green Chartreuse

INSTRUCTIONS
Combine all ingredients in a mixing glass
filled with ice and stir until cold. Strain into a martini glass
and garnish with an orange twist.

---

[*]   Vya refuses to disclose its production process, citing it as a trade secret.

SUTTON CELLARS BROWN LABEL VERMOUTH

THE DOGPATCH, SAN FRANCISCO

If the best description of Vya vermouth is that it exists in a rather ambiguous purgatory, situated between the early-twentieth-century American vermouths that sought to imitate their European ancestors and the new American vermouths that seek to create a style of their own, then Sutton Cellars Brown Label Vermouth deserves credit for taking the first step toward starting the category's revolution. Sutton Cellars was the first vermouth producer to address the problem of the European brands being too bitter, too sweet, and not drinkable on their own, and ultimately in need of a refresher. Here's how it happened.

Check the flats east of Potrero Hill in San Francisco. There are about nine square blocks of what used to be workers' lodges, workshops, brick warehouses, and large industrial public buildings constructed between 1860 and 1945. Locals call this place the Dogpatch. It is one of the few neighborhoods to survive the 1906 earthquake and fire, so it boasts awe-inspiring intact historic industrial surroundings. The old shipyards and pier give it a gritty, manufacturing-turned-hipster-artisan type of vibe. It's right off the T Third line and couldn't be any more different than the tame serenity of the San Joaquin Valley.

Carl Sutton moved there from Sonoma in 1996 and opened up a warehouse winery, immediately making his mark as the prototype California hipster urban vintner. Sutton is a little atypical for a winemaker, though. He's known to rage on weekends, isn't afraid to break up a female-skinhead fistfight, and will not open his winery if he's hung over. He speaks loudly and emphatically about every topic imaginable, including the question of whether the Reinheitsgebot really was a "beer purity law" or just a "war on drugs."** But he's at his loudest when discussing vermouth and other aromatized wines. He's a character. It's unclear if he ever takes off his black T-shirt that says, in white lettering, "Sutton Cellars/Put Some in Your Mouth". His handlebar mustache, even in an age of irony, is worn in a manner that

---

** The Reinheitsgebot was a Bavarian law passed in 1487 mandating the use of only three ingredients in beer production: water, barley, and hops.

suggests complete seriousness. He's a devotee of Patrick McGovern, and he understands the history of botanical infused alcoholic beverages as well as anyone.[130]

In 2009 Sutton had a couple of conversations with local bartenders who were starting to question the lack of quality vermouths. Dolin, the French dry vermouth Eric Seed "discovered" and brought to America from Chambery had just arrived in the Bay Area (and wasn't anywhere else). Carpano Antica Formula, the newly re-produced version of an old Carpano recipe for vermouth with vanilla, was around in limited quantities, but some complained of it being too overpowering—a "vanilla bomb." So, they started looking for an alternative.

Sutton knew that another winemaker, up north by the name of Quady, had released a dry and sweet vermouth ten years earlier, but it wasn't a significant player. Notwithstanding Vya's failure to gain any substantive market share in the prior decade, Sutton believed that a fresh vermouth—one that was made, bottled, and sold within a few months, if not weeks—would get people interested. When he set out to make his vermouth, his first goal was to "make sure it didn't taste like Andy's," which he describes accurately as walking through an alpine/eucalyptus forest just after a spring rain. Sounds idyllic at first blush, but it can be too herbal and bracing for those not accustomed to it. Sutton wanted to create something totally different, something that anyone could relate to.

In late 2009, he created a locally sourced California vermouth in his winery. He called it Sutton Cellars Brown Label Vermouth. He didn't make a lot, but it did find a small and rabid following in San Francisco (the only market it was available for the next few years).

When Sutton submitted an application to have his vermouth formula approved by the United States Tax and Trade Bureau in early 2009, he was told that not a single person had applied for a vermouth formula approval in over a decade. His formula did eventually get approved, and in 2010 he started selling it to select bars around San Francisco, and out of his winery in the Dogpatch.

Sutton's focus was to recognize that most dry vermouths tend to have overly herbal profiles. He wanted to shift the taste toward a more fruit forward and floral flavor profile. Sutton's dry-style vermouth uses a flavor triangle as the base, consisting of fruit, floral, and herbal. To accomplish this triangle he employed seventeen ingredients. It is extremely difficult if not impossible to tease the flavors out of Sutton's vermouth—or Sutton himself, for that matter. The only ingredients he will ever disclose are dried orange peel, chamomile, and rosemary. The first two are macro ingredients, the third is meant to be an underpinning, a suggestion, so as to really downplay the herbal.

Sutton does not disclose what style of wine he uses or the fortifier, something that becomes a bit of an aberration among American vermouth producers. The reason for this secrecy is twofold: as an initial matter, Sutton takes the position that Americans tend to be too varietals fixated; he thinks that focusing on the varietal of his vermouth base plays into this fixation; perhaps more significantly, neither the wine nor the fortifier "are that important to the recipe." The white wine is "really boring" and un-aged brandy is "really neutral."

What we do know is that Sutton starts by adding the neutral brandy to white wine to elevate the alcohol to 17 percent. Once the desired ABV is reached, each individual botanical is soaked in a container appropriate for the volume needed for the recipe. The wine is kept at cellar temperature and never heated. Each botanical is macerated for approximately two weeks before the wine is racked off. Then each separate aromatized wine is blended together. This fresh batch is then blended with an existing "mother batch."[131] The final product is bottled without filtration, a process that the producer argues results in a less manipulated, adulterated vermouth, and is therefore of a higher quality.

═ SUTTON & SODA ═

2 oz. Sutton Cellars Brown Label Vermouth

4 oz. soda water

1 orange peel

INSTRUCTIONS

Pour 2 oz. of Sutton Cellar Brown Label into a
Collins glass filled with ice. Top with soda water and
garnish with a twist of orange peel.

Filtration

Wine geeks can get rather heated over the question of whether filtration decreases the quality of a wine or vermouth. This author doesn't believe that filtration necessarily results in a lesser-quality vermouth; as with all things, it's in the technique. I will provide the facts and let readers come to their own conclusion on this one. Filtration is one technique used for clarification and microbiological stabilization, and was introduced to winemaking only thirty to forty years ago. Filtration clarifies the cloudiness found in some wines. It clarifies by—if you can believe this—removing particles in suspension that cause cloudiness.

Filtration not only clarifies visually but also, by removing suspended particles, can from a sensory standpoint make the fruit characteristics of a wine clearer and more vivid. Since some of these particles are yeast and bacteria, filtration plays an important role in the "microbiological" stability of a wine by eliminating the risk that these microbes will ferment undetectable quantities of sugar (or other food sources) still present after bottling.

For those of you who really want to geek out on this stuff: filtration works by forcing murky wine through a filter bed, usually cellulose fibers, which trap impurities. As the vermouth passes through, the fibers trap particles due to their negative charge and create a sieve-like effect.

IMBUE BITTERSWEET VERMOUTH

WILLAMETTE VALLEY, OREGON

There is a natural tension in storytelling between the ideal, linear story, where one thing builds upon and flows naturally and effortlessly from the previous, and the more realistic, harder-to-tell story, which includes vague edges and crossovers, unsuspecting switchbacks and improbable interlacing such that it becomes deadening to read. Imbue Cellars released a "bittersweet" vermouth in late 2010. Although it appeared that they were following a path that would lead the category into the first linear story, shortly thereafter they steered into a second and blurrier storyline by becoming the country's first vermouth company to release a *non-vermouth aperitif wine*.

Whereas Sutton Cellars lays claim to being the first modern winemaker to produce a true American (Californian) vermouth, three friends from the Willamette Valley in Oregon opened the first modern vermouth company, Imbue Cellars. Imbue was built upon the idea of creating a more modern, drinkable American vermouth. And to their credit, they are the first producers who place an emphasis on both the local nature of their base wine—a Pinot Gris from the Willamette Valley—and their fortifying spirit—an *eau de vie* made from a distillate of the same wine produced by Clear Creek Distillery, aged in American oak barrels. Imbue's creators pride themselves on the simplicity of their formula—just nine botanicals including elderflower, orange peel, sage, and clove—and on it being developed in about five months. They called their vermouth "Bittersweet." It hit store shelves in Portland, Oregon, in late 2010, after Neil Kopplin called Sutton to inquire as to the regulatory hurdles necessary to release a vermouth.

The company was something of a small-business overnight success, in Portland at least. They moved over 100 cases (their first production) in just over three months. Like Vya, however, Imbue struggled to gain a strong foothold outside the local Portland bars, because they kept hearing the same thing from bartenders and beverage directors: they weren't interested in tasting vermouth.

This reticence continued for the next eighteen months despite the fact that *Bon Appetit* named 2010 the year of vermouth. *The New York Times* wrote

in February of that year a feature length article on vermouth titled "Vermouth Takes Its Place on the Rocks," suggesting to its readers that they start drinking Vya and Sutton Cellars straight, noting that Dolin had just started being imported into the country after a 100 year absence and that Noilly Prat was retiring its made-for-export dry vermouth and would start shipping to America what it had kept for its countrymen for the past sixty years. By January 2011, the *Wall Street Journal* had proclaimed that "If you think you don't like vermouth, you're wrong" and finally ran an article instructing its readers to pour their old bottles down the drain, move away from the major brands that were only good for mixing, and try one of the few higher quality vermouths on their own—chilled.

The reach of the *Times* and the *Journal,* however, only extends so far, and even as of July 2012 most Americans still thought of vermouth as toxic waste, though were unable to even describe its base. A panel discussion on American vermouth was held at the Tales of the Cocktail (TOTC) in July 2012 (the first one ever), during which Quady, Sutton, and Kopplin, and Boston bartender Jackson Cannon spoke to a sold-out crowd. Kopplin explained that in his experience, "Even in cocktail bars, you can't put vermouth on a menu. You can call it a fortified wine. You can call a vermouth-heavy cocktail a 'reverse martini.' You can go by brand name. You can call it a 'bittersweet aperitif,' but saying 'vermouth' will sink a cocktail." Quady shared a similar sentiment, noting that his "objective from the very beginning was to make something that people would enjoy drinking straight . . . but so far that doesn't seem to be happening."

After two years on the shelf, Imbue Cellars, the country's first modern vermouth company, was concerned about whether the company could survive. By the time of the TOTC panel, Imbue was just about to release another product with the brand name Petal & Thorn, which is an aromatized, fortified wine that they labeled as an "aperitif wine," not as a vermouth. Someone from the audience of this panel discussion asked Kopplin why the company made that decision. He responded that under United States law, producers are free to call their products either vermouth or aperitif wine. The decision was based purely on "marketing considerations."

He was right, legally. The difference between aperitif wine and vermouth in

United States Definition of Vermouth

In 1960, the U.S. federal government officially defined "vermouth." Under the United States Code of Federal Regulations, "aperitif wine is a class of wine having an alcoholic content of not less than 15 percent . . . compounded from grape wine containing added brandy or alcohol, flavored with herbs and other natural aromatic flavoring materials, with or without the addition of caramel for coloring purposes and possessing the taste, aroma, and characteristic generally attributed to aperitif wine." Vermouth, the Federal Regulations goes on to define, "is a type of aperitif wine compounded from grape wine, having the taste, aroma, and characteristics generally attributed to vermouth . . ."

the United States, like in Europe, is one of a small but important degree. Both products, then, under United States law must be made with a base of grape wine, fortified with brandy, and aromatized with natural flavoring materials. Labeling requirements draw a distinction simply by how they taste. And since Imbue Cellars believed that their product tasted like an aperitif wine and not vermouth, they labeled it as such. They were entirely entitled to do that.

As with all decisions, Imbue's release of a "non-vermouth" aromatized wine had consequences. Specifically, it gave European vermouth producers the ability to push their public relations campaign that Americans did not respect the differences between aperitif wine and vermouth.

But by the summer of 2012, regardless of Imbue's reticence, there was something happening in the vermouth market. Paul Clarke, an internationally renowned cocktails and spirits writer, had gotten into the vermouth story and began seriously looking into it. He published an article in September 2012 titled "American Beauty: Domestic winemakers are doing vermouth their own way." This was a full-length feature in *Imbibe*, America's leading magazine for the spirits industry, insisting that American vermouth was going to be a force to be reckoned with.

Notwithstanding the category's slow start, Vya, Sutton Cellars and Imbue all positioned the category to take off when the time was right.

EL PAPI
MICHAEL NEFF, THE THREE CLUBS, HOLLYWOOD, CA

1 oz. Imbue Bittersweet Vermouth
1 oz. Imbue Petal & Thorn Aperitif Wine
½ oz. Hangar 1 Vodka
½ oz. Ilegal Mezcal

INSTRUCTIONS
Pour ingredients into a mixing glass and stir until cold. Serve up in a cocktail coupe with a thin slice of bitter melon.

Are the American Vermouths Really Vermouth?

The differences between New American and European vermouths are like the differences between humans and bonobos: i.e., they are almost identical, but there are certain, noticeable differences that came about along the evolutionary path. American vermouth producers have taken the idea of vermouth, which has, for the past two hundred years, been defined by European producers, and we have made the next evolutionary step. Evolution, of course, doesn't equal improvement; it refers to adaptation. The difference between the vermouth styles is one of adaptation to a new environment, to new times. They are not necessarily improved versions of vermouth, just more modern ones. In the same way that Vinum Hippocraticum is an early prototype and therefore related to Carpano's vermouth, so are American vermouths the next evolutionary step from traditional vermouth.

There is another reason that the vermouth-must-contain-wormwood position sits a little crooked on the back bar. It is based on the now-discarded Aristotelian model that categories result from lists of defining features. Aristotle believed, and rather persuasively argued, that every category has a very specific definition, with very specific traits. The way our brains get us to this automatic categorization—according to Aristotle—is an analysis of its properties and a comparison with the category definition. For the next two and a half millennium, everyone assumed categories were a matter of logic, and objects were either inside or outside of a category. You're either in or you're out.

Philosopher Ludwig Wittgenstein overthrew 2,000-plus years of thinking about categories with a simple twirl of the umbrella and an asking of the question, "What is a game?" This simple, childlike query completely wrecked the previously unassailable understanding of how the human mind creates categories. What Wittgenstein was getting at was the impossibility of agreeing on a definition of a game that encompassed all the games we play.[132] In other words, for every defining feature, for every characteristic that makes up the definition of a game, there is a counterexample.

Can we define spirits categories by definitions? What about vodka—wouldn't attempting to define vodka fail in the same way that attempting to define games failed? We could say that vodka is a type of alcoholic beverage that is (1) from Russia, (2) distilled from potatoes, (3) flavorless, and (4) meant to be drunk chilled and up. We could say all of these things, and they would be true. And yet—you knew this was coming—Grey Goose isn't from Russia, nor is Tito's, or Svedka. Hangar 1 distills its vodka from grapes. Barr Hill distills theirs from honey. Tuthilltown uses apples. All of these are unquestionably vodkas.

The Old World vermouth producers place a lot of emphasis on their use of historical recipes and on their making "traditional" vermouths, i.e., making vermouth that tastes and smells very similar to all of the other vermouths, based on historical assumptions about how vermouth should be made. There is a lot of virtue in that position, and I am a huge fan of all the European producers that have paved the way for American producers. American vermouth producers, however, pride themselves on being innovators, on creating new styles and flavors of vermouth that simultaneously break away from some recent traditions and return to the original production methods.

If you line up the now thirteen American vermouths and taste them side by side, while you could easily tell that they were in the same category, they all have differences in flavor. Likewise, if you tasted Carpano's original vermouth, you would have likely categorized it as Hippocras, not as wormwood wine, or maybe you would have said it was a good example of Hippocras, and a bad example of wormwood wine. So the first difference is uniqueness of flavor. Atsby Vermouth uses nigella seeds and shitake mushrooms, Uncouth uses beets and eucalyptus and hops, Hammer & Tongs uses turmeric. The philosophy and process is different as well. American producers tend to use higher

quality ingredients and have borrowed the ethos of the craft distilling and slow food movements. American producers use higher-quality base wine and fortifying spirits, and use a much broader botanical palette, and more natural sweeteners. The new breed of American producers also avoid using any flavoring agents or extracts or oils, so they are all producing very high-quality, natural vermouths.

ATSBY VERMOUTH

SOHO, NEW YORK CITY

When I started working on the formula for Atsby Vermouth in 2010, there were no American craft vermouths available in New York City. Sutton Cellars was still just in San Francisco. Imbue hadn't yet launched. And Vya, while around, was not considered a craft vermouth but rather thought of in terms of an imitation of European vermouth made on American soil. Nor were there any quality Italian vermouths available in New York City. The competitive set in my original business plan listed only large European and largely unknown American brands that were always found on the bottom shelf of liquor stores.

I am a lawyer by profession, having graduated with a dual degree in philosophy and history, with no background in spirits or wine other than having drunk a lot of them. I was never a bartender. I was fired from my only waiter job after two weeks. I have always been a little put off by the way some people refer to wines with such perfect, yet esoteric, descriptive terms (an insecurity, obviously).

Prior to my trip to Mont Blanc, my understanding of vermouth was identical to every other American's, best summed up by the British writer Sir Kingsley Amis:

> [Vermouth] consist[s] of wine from inferior districts flavoured with herbs, spices, etc. (a very ancient practice), and lightly stiffened with grape alcohol, with sugar added to the sweet varieties. The Italian (sweet red) sort has a large respectable following and is also popular with alcoholics, perhaps because of its blandness and good value strength against price. The French (dry white) sort is popular with ladies and others who don't really like drinks at all. Chamberyzette is a French vermouth flavoured with wild strawberries, delicious to some, reminding others of whitewash.[133]

Or as described by spirits writer Bruce Watson when tasting traditional big brand vermouths: "syrupy sweet, with notes of film canister . . . tastes like corn syrup served from a metal canteen" and "Franzia mixed with dulce de leche . . .

eye makeup remover with hints of thyme and caramel."[134] That belief was shown to be baseless on my hike around Mt. Blanc.

All of this is to say that I took a more bookish approach to creating Atsby Vermouth. I spent a lot of time studying and thinking about vermouth. I was surprised to discover that there were practically no books on the topic. Even the internet, for all of its wonders, turned out to be less than helpful in this arena. Other than Amerine's annotated bibliography, there were no decent books on the history of vermouth (other than *Il Vermouth di Torino*, the 1907 tract by Arnaldo Strucchi that I was able to read thanks to Google translate, my Nespresso maker, and my ability to type fairly well).

While I'm not a golfer, I have always enjoyed the theory that one shouldn't even think about putting a ball on the ground until the swing has been mastered. So I didn't even think about putting a botanical in wine until I believed I had mastered the record of the product and the ideas behind it. This took well over eighteen months.

When I tried that glass of vermouth back in Courmayeur, Piedmont, I was actually in the birthplace of vermouth. I used that fact as the starting point of my study. And here is what I came up with: vermouth, I began to believe, has a way of bridging time, making the drinker feel simultaneously historical yet modern. It may have something to do with vermouth representing the evolution of how humans have been enjoying alcohol for the past several thousand years. When you read about the history of alcohol consumption, you see that people from every continent (except North America!) have a long history of drinking wines, either from grapes or other fermented carbohydrates, that have been infused with various botanicals and sweetened, often using honey or whatever natural sweetening agent was indigenous to the area.

But the story of vermouth is also the story of modernity. Antonio Benedetto Carpano is universally acknowledged as the inventor of modern vermouth. As I sat at my kitchen table—when I wasn't holed up in the library—I began to understand exactly what Carpano did that was so revolutionary. Carpano's genius stemmed from two innovative principles: the first was making his aromatized, fortified wine with high quality wines such as Moscato from Piedmont and strong wines from southern Italy and Sicily. No one had done that before. His other stroke of genius was using numerous botanicals (supposedly over fifty) so that no one could really identify the flavor of any one herb or spice and then sweetening them just the right amount to create a perfectly balanced drink that was intended to be drunk on its own.

The more I learned about vermouth—that it was traditionally made with a high-quality base wine and an assortment of any botanicals I could dream of, fortified with any fruit brandy I could lay my hands on; that the European producers used to make their vermouths in this style but began taking shortcuts in the 1960s—the more I wanted to create my own vermouth in the original Carpano style.

In September 2012, Atsby Vermouth released two expressions: an amber version, Amberthorn, that contains twenty-one botanicals, and the slightly sweeter bourbon-hued Armadillo Cake, with thirty-two different botanicals—both differing from the traditional European styles.

Atsby Vermouth is made by cold steeping all of the botanicals together at the same time in cellar temperature, steel-tank-fermented Chardonnay. The botanicals are left to macerate for about a month, after which they are removed and the apple brandy is added to both aromatized wines. Raw summer honey is added to the Amberthorn and caramel from dark Indian Muscovado sugar is added to the Armadillo Cake. Both vermouths are then left to rest for about six months before filtering and bottling.

DOUBLE BARREL

1 oz. Atsby Armadillo Cake Vermouth
1 oz. Atsby Amberthorn Vermouth
1 oz. rye

INSTRUCTIONS
Pour all ingredients into a mixing glass and stir 10 times.
Strain into a rocks glass, served up.

UNCOUTH VERMOUTH

RED HOOK, BROOKLYN

If I have taken the position that vermouth is the story of trade routes, Bianca Miraglia of Uncouth Vermouth takes the opposite approach. To Miraglia, vermouth's story is the story of the wines being made during Hippocrates' time, like those described by Pliny the Elder. Whereas Atsby sought to make vermouth in the original, post–trade route, pre–World War II style, Uncouth sought to make vermouth the way aromatized, fortified wines were made prior to the trade routes, when it was only possible to aromatize wine with herbs that were found within several miles of where it was being produced.

Everything in Uncouth Vermouths is hyperlocal. The mugwort and rosehips are among 30 different botanicals that are foraged—handpicked by Miraglia, shoved into the trunk of her hatchback, and driven back to her production facility in Red Hook, Brooklyn. The feverfew, sumac, and lemon balm are grown by her mother, an internationally lauded orchid grower. All of the other botanicals are grown at a local farm, never farther than forty miles from New York City. The products are not sweetened—other than by the wine's natural sweetener, which results from the residue after fermentation. Some do contain fruit, and they are fortified with a grape brandy.

Uncouth Vermouth should have launched commercially about two months after Atsby in late October 2012, but Hurricane Sandy abolished the Red Hook winery where Miraglia was manufacturing it. Red Hook took one of the worst beatings during the storm, when Pier 41 and Liberty Warehouse for all intents and purposes became part of the Atlantic Ocean. The company recovered, and in January 2013, Uncouth Vermouth launched its first three seasonal varieties: Beet Eucalyptus, Apple Mint, and Pear Ginger. Within the next year, Uncouth went on to release a Butternut Squash, Serrano Chile Lavender, Wild Raspberry, Cherry, Rhubarb, and shortly thereafter Miraglia released a dry-hopped vermouth, and a wildflower vermouth in 2015. Uncouth now produces more than ten seasonal vermouths.

The first trick to making Uncouth Vermouth is creating sweet vermouths that do not use sugar. The secret to this is to use very late season and botrytized wine.

Uncouth Vermouths are each made completely differently, though they all are made similarly to the ancient tradition of brewing tea. Miraglia very gently heats her base wine and steeps the botanicals. Depending on the varietal, she will add components at different times of the production process. For many of them, she will do a double infusion. That is, she will do a single maceration infusion using a wine base of either a Chardonnay-Viognier blend from the North Fork of Long Island, or a Riesling or Catawba grapes from the Finger Lakes. Then she will do a second maceration to bring out the dominant flavors. While she does not use any sugars, chunks of whole fruit or juiced vegetables such as beets or butternut squash are added to either the first infusion, or immediately prior to bottling, to give it some natural fructose. Uncouth Vermouths are fortified right before bottling, which is very unusual. The reason for this late fortification is to allow the transformation caused by the infusion to continue until it exactly where Miraglia wants it. The fortifying agent stops the conversion, and preserves it as is. Like Sutton Cellars Vermouths, Uncouth Vermouths are also not filtered before bottling. They are made in stainless steel—her biggest batch is 55 gallons.

THE VERMOUTH MARTINI

2¼ oz. Apple Mint vermouth
¾ oz. New York Distilling Company Dorothy Parker American Gin

---

INSTRUCTIONS:
Pour both ingredients into a mixing glass
filled halfway with ice. Stir until very cold, strain into a glass,
and garnish with a lemon rind.

Botrytized Wine

As any wine geek will tell you, for wines to have natural sugar, they need heat. This is why wines from hotter climates like California or Portugal tend to be sweeter. To let the sugar really come out, the sun must hit the grape directly, turning the acid into sugar. To get the sweetness in a wine from grapes in colder climates, one must pick the grapes later in the season. This is why when you eat a green grape from early in the season it is really acidic. If it sits on the vine, then the acid turns to brix, or sugar. Botrytized grapes develop what is called a healthy rot or the "noble rot." They look like fuzzy raisins when you pick them. The producer must rehydrate the grapes and then press them.

MORE BOLD NEW FLAVORS

Sales of artisanal vermouth in the United States skyrocketed in 2014, making vermouth one of the fastest-growing categories in the United States wine trade. Since Uncouth Vermouth was released in January 2013, dozens of vermouth producers have hit the shelves. This includes Tad Seestedt's Ransom Vermouth, which is the first American vermouth to use wormwood and to break free from the age-old tradition of keeping vermouth recipes secret: Ransom lists all of its ingredients right on the label. Hammer & Tongs, created by Patrick Taylor, takes an entirely new angle on vermouth by focusing on spices from North and West Africa and on tree resins from antiquity. Channing Daughters, the successful Long Island winery run by winemaker Chris Tracey, released several formulas in 2013. Then came Massican, Interrobang, Matthiasson, and Harris Bridge Vineyard's Timber Sweet Vermouth. Some of these brands continue to innovate and others are actually imitative of other American brands, demonstrating that the industry has come into itself.

For three generations it was embarrassing to put vermouth in your cocktail. That scene in *Mad Men* when Roger Sterling yells "whoa, whoa easy on the vermouth" is telling of how generations thought about the product. What all of these brands have done, by working independently and collectively, is manage to reinvigorate a category that had been completely dead for sixty years. And now, the statement that vermouth is the next big thing in the spirits world hardly needs support anymore. On December 12, 2013, Fox News published a national article titled "The Hot New Hooch, American Vermouth." *Tasting Panel,* a widely regarded industry magazine, circulated a long feature titled "The Truth About Vermouth." *New York* magazine printed a beautiful centerfold photo of ten new vermouths to hit the shelves in the past sixteen months for the story "Vermouth's Bittersweet Revenge."

For the first time in generations, *Wine Spectator* ran a full length feature article on the product, "A New Approach to Vermouth," in which the venerable Jack Bettridge explained how vermouth got its reputation back, detailing that it's not the European producers but in fact the American craft producers who have been driving the excitement in this once forgotten category. Bettridge wrote that the new vermouths have been made "necessary" for bartenders, and that drinkers worldwide should "take notice of the explosively flavorful, reinvented versions."[135]

Alice Feiring, a well-known wine writer, wrote a multi-page feature for the *New York Times* on how exciting the American vermouth category is right now.[136] Similarly, *Wine Enthusiast Magazine* reports that the new vermouths exist to "upgrade" the cocktails produced in bars today, highlighting how the new players to the market are infusing energy into cocktail bars across the country.[137] The list could go on. There have been hundreds of articles written about vermouth since 2013, while there were a mere handful written between 1960 and 2012. All of them agree: vermouth is the thing to be drinking today.

Vermouth has gained traction not only in the press but also with the two key target groups in any on-the-rise spirit's ascent: those who serve and those who regularly imbibe (the majority of whom are Millennials). Many of the most well-respected cocktail artists, such as NYC's Sother Teague from Amor Y Amargo and Franky Marshall from The Dead Rabbit, and Chicago's Josh Williams of Girl & the Goat to name just a few, have created cocktail menus that feature drinks with ratios that favor vermouth, celebrating the unique, slightly herbal, slightly sweet, slightly bitter qualities of the new American brands as well as the "true" classic recipes of American cocktail culture before Prohibition.[138] Charles Joly, formerly of the Aviary in Chicago and winner of the Diageo World Class 2014 competition for best bartender in the world, demoed a vermouth cocktail with Atsby Vermouth at the Los Angeles Food & Wine Festival main stage in 2014; the recipe was later featured in a full-length article in *SAVEUR* magazine on American Vermouths.[139]

Not only is it common now to see brand ambassadors for new American vermouths sampling products in local wine and spirits shops across the country, but these spirits have taken industry trade shows by storm. During the 2014 Manhattan Cocktail Classic, an annual celebration of cocktail products and trends in the city most steeped in vermouth history, the panel on "The Rise of Artisanal Vermouth in America" presented to a sold-out crowd, while the panel hosted by Martini & Rossi to counteract the American vermouth resurgence had a significant number of empty chairs.[140]

Vermouth hasn't excited just bartenders but the wine community as well. Two of our country's twenty-nine Masters of Wine, Jennifer Simonetti-Bryan and Christy Canterbury, have recently shown support for craft American vermouths in industry publications and tastings, recognizing their value as complex, sippable wines rather than as mere ingredients in complex cocktails. Never before in history has a Master of Wine approved of a vermouth for drinking.

Somewhat amazingly, it took only two years for the anti-vermouth mindset to do a 180-degree turn. This happened overnight, in branding time, due to the proliferation of American vermouth brands, the infiltration of those brands into modern drinking culture, and the rising interest of print and social media in the fascinating spirit.

This very recent interest extends beyond America. Spain has seen vermouth take over as *the* national drink (usurping the reign of gin and tonic).[141] They call it *fer vermut* in Catalonian or *hacer vermut* in Spanish ("to have vermouth"), and it is considered more than a mere drink—it is a distinctive ritual that everyone under thirty-five performs daily. In the past two years, the ancestral home of vermouth, Italy, began exporting new formulas like Contratto, Cocchi, and Carpano Bianco, while their French neighbor just across the Alpine Mountains, Noilly Prat, created an all-new "Extra Dry" formula especially for the American market in 2012.[142] Craft vermouth producers like Regal Rogue from Australia, Yzaguirre from Spain, The Collector from England, Belsazar from Germany, and on and on were not far behind.

Vermouth pairing and tasting classes have taken off in New York City and other metropolitan areas. In 2014, Food Network star chef Nikki Martin cooked for an exclusive group of twenty-five people, pairing vermouth with her dishes and in specialty cocktails. Vermouth-centric cocktails-and-cheese classes are now bimonthly staples of the schedule at Murray's Cheese, New York's oldest cheese shop and one of the most respected cheese schools in the country. Some of their most acclaimed wine instructors choose to include vermouths in their broader wine-and-cheese-pairing classes.[143]

Yet despite all of this tremendous success and excitement about vermouth in the press and among many bartenders, the complete overhaul of its image is still a long way off; much work remains to be done. This is an exciting and interesting time to be alive, and to have at our fingertips access to such well-made vermouths, both for drinking on their own and for elevating cocktails, is an experience to honor and respect.

While there are now over a dozen American vermouth producers, even more are needed so that we fill up the store shelves. There is strength in numbers, and every new brand that comes onto the market is a welcome addition. I urge all the people interested in getting into vermouth production to do it, and ask only that they commit to making vermouths with new, unique flavor profiles. The United States has the best laws in the world to support this category. Our laws allow for limitless possibilities with flavor, tastes, and aromas, yet maintain the integrity of the product by *precluding* the use of neutral grain spirits as the fortifying agent, and instead permitting the use of any brandy.

The most important thing for American vermouth producers going forward is to protect vermouth from the axes that hack. In other words, never let vermouth revert back to a mass-produced, undifferentiated, industrial product made for mixing. The race to the bottom that America witnessed after WWII is a stain on this great category, and having lived through it once we should never return to it. There is such an infinite palette of flavors, tastes, and aromas and so much uncharted territory that there should never be a need for vermouths to be made that taste like another brands. Americans have now reached a point where we are ready for bold new flavors and ideas. We are getting into bitters and "unusual" tastes, and vermouth should be at the forefront of introducing ever changing, radical, and delicious new flavors from now until, well, forever.

chapter four

VERMOUTH COCKTAILS

It is possible to read almost every pre-Prohibition cocktail book in one day, if you do nothing else that day. Like most everything else in this world though, just because it's possible doesn't mean it's advisable. In fact if you can avoid it, I'd recommend it. They are, on a whole, tedious and impenetrable. Many of them list hundreds of cocktails, one after another, with no immediately apparent rhyme or reason. Most of the cocktails are differentiated only by a dash of this or that, and just as many list dozens of names for the same exact cocktail, without bothering to note why one has a name that's different than another. One of these books lists no fewer than fifteen "different" cocktails, all of which call for one part sweet vermouth, one part dry vermouth, and one part gin. The only saving grace for the pack are the forewords written by David Wondrich and Paul Clarke in recent reprints.

> *"In drinking, our aim must be enjoyment, not inebriation."*
>
> **—The Only William,**
> *The Flowing Bowl: When and What to Drink*[144]

What these books lack in style and flair, however, they more than make up for in historical significance and practical advice. They help tell the story of vermouth as the cocktail's most important ingredient, and they contain drinks that have managed to scratch American's drinking itch for the last century and a half.

What these cocktail books don't do is refer to anything as a "vermouth cocktail" (except the actual "Vermouth Cocktail"). That's a recent phrase, and one I don't like but feel inclined to use, for now, to describe cocktails where vermouth makes up the base spirit. Cocktails that used vermouth as the base spirit, modifier, or as the drink itself were not separated out from any other spirit, liquor, or cordial in any of the original late-nineteenth-century cocktail books; they just appear right in the assembly line, as if they fit in with rye and Old Tom gin like old, grade school pals.

The following, then, are vermouth cocktails. They are cocktails that have a base of vermouth and employ spirits as the modifier. The secret to using quality vermouth in a cocktail is to use more vermouth than spirit; otherwise you risk washing all the nuanced flavors away with the heavier-proof spirit. Cocktails made in this fashion, I think you will find, are even more satisfying than the more recent traditional, spirit-heavy cocktails.

A Note on Recipe Construction

As you'll notice, with limited exceptions, these cocktails suggest the use of American vermouth rather than the standard Italian and French brands. This is based on several considerations.

First, bartenders have been trained in how to use the European brands for the past fifty years, and knowledge about how to use them has trickled down to most drinkers.

Second, with the major influx of quality vermouth brands, most with totally different flavor profiles now on the market, I would be remiss if I suggested that we should still be using the same old brands with the same standard flavor profiles. We should celebrate that we are living in a time of unprecedented innovation and take full advantage of it.

Finally, these cocktails all call for a majority of vermouth. I have found, and most every bartender I have ever interviewed agrees, that the imported sweet vermouths are too syrupy and sweet to compose the majority of a cocktail. Dry-style vermouths, on the other hand, tend to lack the distinctive flavor profile or have the volume to carry a cocktail.

For these reasons, standard European brands are still best used as they have advertised themselves, as modifiers, whereas the new brands that have broken from these flavor characteristics will make a better vermouth cocktail.

BRUNCH COCKTAILS

Brunch, that luxurious, elegant meal, first found a foothold in New Orleans right before the turn of the twentieth century, when a German immigrant named Madame Begue served up a second breakfast to French merchants. It was New York City, however, that made it into the institution that it is today. The infamous Oscar of the Waldorf-Astoria first started serving morning cocktails and lavish meals with staples of eggs Benedict, *omelette aux fines herbes*, and poached eggs with truffles.

While traditional brunch cocktails consist of champagne, fruit juices, and simple spirits such as vodka, the cocktails here all aim at cutting down on the percentage of fruit juice and including more flavors from the vermouth.

DOUBLE ROCKS

INGREDIENTS

1½ oz. Atsby Amberthorn Vermouth

½ oz. Absolut Smokey Tea Vodka (or vodka infused with Lapsang souchong)

¾ oz. homemade ginger syrup

½ oz. fresh lemon juice

1 piece candied ginger

INSTRUCTIONS

Add all ingredients to a mixing tin, shake with ice, and strain into a double rocks glass filled with fresh ice. Garnish with candied ginger.

CORNELIA

MS. FRANKY MARSHALL, NYC

In the summer of 1982, writer Calvin Trillin noted in an article in the *New Yorker* that "a place in Greenwich Village called the Cornelia Street Café [seems] to be going about its business under the assumption that the village is still the Village."[145] Which explains why a few years later Jonathan Goodman called for the attention of "aging romantics, young couples intent on an intimate evening, and literati in possession of a discriminating palate" to Cornelia Street. My wife and I took our kids to brunch there recently, and after a decade still nothing has changed.

The Cornelia cocktail is an eye-opener, perfect for starting off a weekend morning. The smoky flavor from the Lapsang souchong is reminiscent of waking up in a strange apartment the second hot day of summer. The lemon juice and ginger liqueur open up the airways and allow for easier breathing.

WINE   CHAMPAGNE FLUTE

MONOSABIO

GARRY SEVERIN, THE LAMB'S CLUB

The Monosabio is the red scarf worn by bull-fighters' assistants. This is a riff on the cocktail called Death in the Afternoon, named after Hemingway's book on bullfighting. When Garry Severin served this at the Manhattan Cocktail Classic in 2013, he said he hoped this would help "kill the tyranny of the mimosa." I can only hope that happens.

INGREDIENTS

2 oz. dry vermouth

1 oz. grapefruit juice

¾ oz. Aperol

½ oz. lime juice

½ oz. lemon juice

1 raspberry or grapefruit round

INSTRUCTIONS

Shake all ingredients in a cocktail shaker and pour into a wine glass or champagne flute. Then top with Prosecco (or other sparkling wine) and garnish with a grapefruit slice or single red raspberry.

SUGGESTED VERMOUTHS

Atsby Amberthorn

Imbue Bittersweet

Ransom Dry

Sutton Cellar Brown Label

Uncouth Apple Mint

SUNDAY MORNING

PAM WIZNITZER, NYC

PINT

Beer cocktails have become all the rage lately, and it's not a surprising trend. With literally hundreds of visionary craft brews on the market, why not pair them with spirits and fruit juices? This might be the perfect Sunday morning cocktail; it contains everything that is good in this world: vermouth, whiskey, liquor, and beer. You can vary the garnish with the seasons: blackberries in late spring, apricot in the early summer, lime for the hottest months, and cherry in the fall.

INGREDIENTS

1½ oz. Armadillo Cake Vermouth

1 oz. Stranahans Colorado Whiskey

¾ oz. lime juice

½ oz. apricot liqueur

½ oz. honey water (equal parts honey and water)

Hefeweizen beer

INSTRUCTIONS

Pour the vermouth, whiskey, lime juice, apricot liqueur, and honey water into a cocktail shaker with three ice cubes and shake a few times. Strain into a pint glass filled with ice and top with Hefeweizen beer.

COUPE

CORPSE REVIVER #9

INGREDIENTS

1½ oz. Uncouth Dry Hopped Vermouth

1 oz. London dry gin

¾ oz. fresh squeezed lemon juice

½ oz. Cointreau

1 dash absinthe

INSTRUCTIONS

Place all ingredients in cocktail shaker filled with ice, shake vigorously, and strain into a coupe glass, and add a lemon twist garnish.

Besides having one of the best names of any cocktail, the Corpse Reviver is perhaps also the most helpful. It is, as the name suggests, the perfect hair of the dog. Perfect for a very early breakfast following a proper evening filled with completely appropriate behavior, if you know what I mean.

COUPE

INGREDIENTS

½ oz Atsby Armadillo Cake

½ oz Atsby Amberthorn

½ oz freshly squeezed lemon juice

1 oz gin (Tanqueray Rangpur)

¾ oz salted caramel sauce

Kaffir leaves

Chartreuse

INSTRUCTIONS

Combine all ingredients into a mixing glass and stir 40 rotations. Strain into a coupe glass. Add 6 dashes of chartreuse and garnish with grapefruit zest and Kaffir leaf.

BRONX COCKTAIL

PIERRE-HUGUES MAROIS, MONTREAL

The Bronx Cocktail enjoyed serious success in the early 1900s before it fell into oblivion, likely because bartenders used to much juice and wrecked the balance. The problem, most people agree, was with the addition of orange juice, and too much of it.

Thankfully, bartenders are giving this old cocktail a serious makeover. When I was up in Montreal during the freezing winter of 2015, the guys over at Bishop and Bagg hosted a Bronx Cocktail competition. True to form, the only rules of the game were that the cocktail had to resemble the original and couldn't stray too far from its essence. The winner that night was the talented and humble Pierre-Hugues Marois. After holding his winning arm high in the air that night, I twisted it until he disclosed his secrets.

VERMOUTH & SODA (OR EVERYBODY KNOWS)

ROCKS   COLLINS

Vermouth and soda has been a classic drink for about as long as there has been vermouth and sparkling water. If you want to move from simple to spectacular, switch out the sparkling water for Champagne, Prosecco or sparkling wine. For another layer of complexity and deliciousness add a few drops of simple syrup, honey syrup, or a fruit puree. Vary the garnish with the seasons. You can use allspice, dates, lemon, ginger, pear, raspberry, watermelon, or apple depending on your tastes.

INGREDIENTS

2½ oz. vermouth

4 oz. soda water

Twist of orange (or lemon, or seasonal fruit)

INSTRUCTIONS

Pour 2½ oz. of quality vermouth into a rocks or Collins glass and top with sparkling water. Garnish with seasonal fruit.

SUGGESTED VERMOUTHS

Atsby

Imbue Bittersweet

Ransom

Sutton Cellars Brown Label

Uncouth Wildflower

Vya Dry

VARIATION

Try swapping out the plain sparkling water for a specialty soda (the line of Pellegrino sodas work particularly well).

COCKTAIL

INGREDIENTS

1¼ oz. Atsby Amberthorn
Vermouth

½ oz. mango nectar

½ oz. pear nectar

½ oz. mild Jamaican curry
powder

½ oz. fresh orange juice

¼ oz. fresh lemon juice

INSTRUCTIONS

Combine all ingredients in a
shaker filled with ice, shake
vigorously, and strain into a
martini glass. Garnish with a
pear slice, orange round, or
cubed mango.

1,001 NIGHTS
ALEX OTT

Alex Ott, the "sorcerer of shaken and stirred," created this exquisite drink as an "appetizer, aphrodisiac, and stimulant." When Alex isn't formulating perfume recipes for Tom Ford or creating drinks for astronauts working on the international space station (seriously), he's staring at his wall thinking of other out-of-this-world cocktails. Alex speaks often on the importance of only ingesting food and drink that have some positive health benefit, and for that reason, he is particularly pulled toward vermouths. The liberal quantities of fruit juices in this cocktail pair perfectly with the vermouth, and the addition of the curry—with all its antioxidant properties—insures that your body is replenishing everything it lost from the night before.

APERITIF COCKTAILS

When done right, aperitif cocktails are extraordinary. They're different than the kinds of cocktail you traditionally think of, drinks that are intended to be taken back quickly. Aperitif cocktails are intended to be sipped lazily while you start to unwind from the day's work. The Spanish know how to aperitif; they call it *fer vermut* ("to do vermouth"), and it is a distinctive ritual with its own set of rules. Aperitif cocktails should be drunk at the end of the afternoon, or just possibly at the start of the evening. They are intended to stimulate, and to get you ready for the evening. If possible, they should be drunk with light snacks, olives, nuts, cheese, charcuterie; everything should be easy about these cocktails.

ROCKS

WHITE NEGRONI

The White Negroni is exactly what you think it is: a Negroni with all the red ingredients swapped out for lighter-colored ones. It uses dry vermouth instead of sweet and a gentian liqueur instead of a bitter orange one. Try swapping out the Suze for Salers or Lillet for a slightly lighter drink.

INGREDIENTS

2 oz. dry vermouth

½ oz. Greenhook Ginsmiths Gin

½ oz. Suze bitters

1 lemon peel

INSTRUCTIONS

Pour all ingredients into a mixing glass and stir until they are very cold. Strain into a rocks glass. Garnish with a twist of lemon.

SUGGESTED VERMOUTHS

Atsby Amberthorn

Ransom Dry

Sutton Cellars Brown Label

Uncouth Apple Mint

COUPE

INGREDIENTS

1¼ oz. sweet vermouth

1 oz. hibiscus-tea-infused Scotch

1 oz. chamomile grappa

2 dashes orange bitters

Hibiscus flower

INSTRUCTIONS

Pour all ingredients into a mixing glass and stir until they are cold. Strain into a cocktail coupe, and garnish with an orange or lemon twist.

SUGGESTED VERMOUTHS

Atsby Armadillo Cake

Hammer & Tongs Sac'Résine or L'Afrique

Carpano Antica Formula

Vya Sweet

TEA TIME

GARRY SEVERIN, THE LAMB'S CLUB

Garry Severin's Tea Time manages what many people believe is impossible: it makes Scotch play nice with other ingredients. The secret, it turns out, is infusing the Scotch with hibiscus tea. This, along with the chamomile grappa and a good dose of vermouth, pulls the drink together in a way that highlights the vermouth, and accents its unusual flavors.

A SPORT AND A PASTIME

JOSH SONTAG, HEAD BARTENDER, THE
BRESLIN AT THE ACE HOTEL, NYC

COUPE

The Koran instructs that this world is but a
sport and a pastime, a line that inspired nov-
elist James Salter to author a book by that
name about the feverish love affair between
an uncommitted college dropout and a young
French girl. It's the type of story that allows
you to sleep easier at night, just knowing that
some people might have such experiences,
even if you're not one of them. This cocktail drinks with all the flavor, movement, and
intensity of a good love affair. It leaves you
wanting another.

INGREDIENTS

2 oz. dry vermouth

½ oz. Cherry Heering

½ oz. fresh lime juice

INSTRUCTIONS

Pour all ingredients into a
mixing glass filled with ice,
and stir 20 times. Strain into
coupe. Garnish with a cherry
and lime wheel.

SUGGESTED VERMOUTHS

Sutton Cellars Brown Label

Ransom

Atsby Amberthorn

Uncouth Apple Mint

COCKTAIL

INGREDIENTS

2 oz. Bianco vermouth

¾ oz. Square One Vodka

¼ oz. pear liqueur

1 pear slice

INSTRUCTIONS

Pour all ingredients into a mixing glass and stir until almost freezing. Strain into a chilled cocktail glass. Garnish with expressed orange oils. Serve with a side of Marcona almonds.

SUGGESTED VERMOUTHS

Imbue Bittersweet

Martini Bianco

Dolin Bianco

PALE END OF DAY

Vodka has gotten a bad rap lately, but this is mostly a function of the backlash against brands being overly branded, overly marketed, and supported by stories that have jumped the shark. Vodka isn't bad. (I'm thinking of shots of Russian Standard with tins of Beluga caviar during New Year's Eve 2001 in Saint Petersburg and wondering how anyone could suggest vodka in and of itself is bad.) The secret to using vodka is to not rely on it as the main ingredient, but rather to use it as a higher-proof spirit that can push up the flavors of other spirits it's mixed with. This is exactly what this cocktail does; the vodka enhances the vermouth and liqueur. It is slightly sweeter than these other cocktails, but in a good way.

ROCKS

ON THE RADIO

On the Radio is a perfect drink to make as a punch and serve at a party. It's filled with unusual but complementary flavors, and is reminiscent of the classic vermouth cocktail, but where aquavit is added as well. Most importantly, it can hold up to having a large chunk of ice in the middle of it, slowly melting and diluting it.

INGREDIENTS

36 oz. Atsby Amberthorn

12 oz. Linie Aquavit

2 oz. Maraschino liqueur

10 dashes orange bitters

INSTRUCTIONS

Pour all ingredients into a large punch bowl filled with one very large chunk of ice and mix slowly until blended. Add hibiscus and other edible flowers to garnish the bowl. Ladle into rocks glasses without a garnish.

MODERN COCKTAILS

These cocktails are a new breed created by some of America's most talented bartenders. They represent the best of what today's cocktails are doing to maintain the quality and integrity of proper cocktails served as they are meant to be.

SHAFER'S EUREKA

JEREMIAH BLAKE, HOLLAND HOUSE
BAR + REFUGE, NASHVILLE, TN

SNIFTER

Shafer's Eureka was the name of one of the concert saloons on Broadway south of Houston during the 1860s. The use of chamomile tea here plays beautifully off of the floral components of the vermouths and also blends and tames the bourbon. The resulting drink is reminiscent of sitting in a gaslit basement saloon, surrounded by prizefighters and tattoo artists dressed in their Sunday best and not having a care in the world.

INGREDIENTS

1¾ oz. dry-style vermouth

¾ oz. bourbon

1¼ oz. chamomile tea

Grapefruit bitters

INSTRUCTIONS

Pour all ingredients into a mixing glass filled with ice and stir 20 times. Strain into a brandy snifter.

SUGGESTED VERMOUTHS

Atsby Amberthorn

Ransom

Sutton Cellar Brown Label

Uncouth Wildflower

ROCKS   COUPE

SPRING MANHATTAN

JOSH SONTAG, BRESLIN LOBBY BAR,
ACE HOTEL, NYC

INGREDIENTS

1 oz. Maker's Mark bourbon

1 oz. Armadillo Cake

1 oz. Pimm's

3 dashes peach bitters

1 peach slice

INSTRUCTIONS

Pour all ingredients into a mixing glass and stir until cold. Strain into a rocks or coupe glass, served up or over ice. Garnish with a peach slice or orange peel.

This drink has been one of the all-time top-selling cocktails at the Breslin lobby bar at the Ace Hotel in NYC. When Josh first created it he explained how skeptical he was that it would work or that anyone would order it. Two weeks later he called to tell me that people were ordering this drink three or four at a time. The lower proof and high flavor profile permits for this sort of ordering without any excessive drinking.

RUM DIARY

Having lived in Matanzas, Cuba, toward the end of that country's "special period" in the 1990s, I had my fair share of glasses of Havana Club with a Cohiba. It is only fitting that I would find a way to combine rum, vermouth, and tobacco for a perfect early evening drink. Now that the United States is working to normalize its relationship with Cuba, getting these ingredients should be much easier. I hope the legality of the ingredients won't dampen their flavor, as I've only ever made this with illegal ingredients.

ROCKS

INGREDIENTS

1½ oz. Armadillo Cake Vermouth

1 oz. aged rum (Havana Club from Cuba is the best)

¼ oz. tobacco syrup

2 dashes bitters

INSTRUCTIONS

Build in mixing glass over ice, stir cold, strain into a glass of your choice, no garnish. (There were no fancy cocktail glasses in Cuba in 1998.)

TOBACCO SYRUP INSTRUCTIONS

To make tobacco syrup, add 3½ oz. of pipe tobacco to one quart of simple syrup made with demerara sugar, and let it steep at 170 degrees Fahrenheit for 30 minutes. Allow to cool and strain into a glass mason jar and refrigerate.

ORCHARD IN MANHATTAN

SOTHER TEAGUE, AMOR Y AMARGO

COUPE

You know you're listening to a talented guitar player when you can recognize the specific musician in one or two chords. These are people who have so much personality that they are immediately identifiable by their talent and confidence. Some bartenders are like this, and Sother Teague, head bartender of Amor Y Amargo, is one of these bartenders. He makes his cocktails like a master musician, that is, one sip and you know he has made it. This cocktail bears his signature, full of flavorful ingredients that do not overpower one another. Rather, they all play harmoniously together. Drinking it makes you imagine sitting in an apple orchard in the fall while a talented stranger strums a 12-string guitar.

INGREDIENTS

1¼ oz. Cocchi Vermouth

1¼ oz. Louis Royer Force 53 VSOP Cognac

½ oz. apple brandy

½ oz. Becherovka

1 dash of apple bitters

INSTRUCTIONS

Pour all ingredients into a mixing glass and stir 40 times, or until cold. Strain into a coupe, garnish with an apple slice.

ROCKS

THE SUN ALSO RISES

JOSH SONTAG, BRESLIN LOBBY BAR, ACE HOTEL, NYC

INGREDIENTS

1½ oz. Atsby Amberthorn Vermouth

1 oz. New York Distilling Company Dorothy Parker American Gin

½ oz. Baines Pacharan

Expressed orange

INSTRUCTIONS

Pour all ingredients into a mixing glass and stir 22 times. Strain into a rocks glass and give a heavy spritz of expressed orange.

I needed a cocktail for the launch of the 3.1 Phillip Lim spring 2014 collection at Saks Fifth Avenue. They wanted a cocktail that would match the "vibe" of Lim's collection and the season it was meant to represent. Nothing can be more fun than thinking of a cocktail to match a wardrobe. This collection happened to be a cross between New York City (the low-cut V-necked T-shirts read i heart nueva york) and a field of wildflowers. The cocktail was easy: 95 percent New York ingredients, with a touch of a Spanish liqueur. We handed it out for free at Saks on 51st Street in Manhattan and had lines weaving through the collection all night long.

LATE-NIGHT COCKTAILS

Late-night cocktails are drinks that should be made after midnight, when you've been out for a while or maybe just started late. The idea is that you want a drink packed with flavor but low on alcohol, so you can keep going like a bunny, whether in the comfort of your own home or out and about on the town.

CORDIAL

INGREDIENTS

2 oz. sweet vermouth

¾ oz. London dry gin

¼ oz. Fernet-Branca

1 orange peel

INSTRUCTIONS

Pour all ingredients into a mixing glass filled with ice and stir until on the verge of freezing. Strain into a small cordial or sake coupe. Garnish with a raspberry in the spring and summer, or a fig in the fall and winter.

SUGGESTED VERMOUTHS

Atsby Armadillo Cake

Dolin Rouge

Ransom Sweet

HANKY-PANKY

Sadly, the naming of cocktails has been, by most accounts, a fanciful endeavor that involved very little forethought or justification. When I first heard the name of this cocktail, I'll admit to getting aroused on the name alone. It ignites in me a yearning for the salacious tale behind its name. Three bartenders caught doing an around-the-world on top of the bar by the owner? A couple of patrons caught standing in the bathroom? Are you ready? Here it is: when Ada Coleman served a patron one in the Savoy Hotel, he shouted out "By jove! That is the real hanky-panky!"[146] And so Ada named the cocktail the "Hanky-Panky." (I swear that is the entire story.)

Terrible way to name the cocktail, but that doesn't mean your nights drinking it should end as lackluster.

NOTES ON CONSTRUCTION AND DRINKING

This cocktail must be served very cold, and must be drunk just as cold. Once it begins to warm up, the overwhelming flavors of the fernet begin to take over. I recommend mixing a batch up drinking out of a sake glass, while keeping the remaining cocktail cold by placing it into a carafe on ice.

THE MUSEUM OF INNOCENCE

ROCKS

I created this cocktail for the launch party of the exotic and limited-edition Amouage Fate for Men, a cologne only found in a handful of shops throughout the world. I was asked to create a cocktail that would match this cologne, which has beautiful top notes of absinthe and mandarin, with base notes of anise. Atsby Amberthorn Vermouth played in perfectly for this, as it is already redolent with anise and mandarin. With the added absinthe and Malört, the resulting cocktail matched the perfume perfectly. The name is intended to pay homage to the perfumery and atelier MiN, a hidden jewel just south of the gas station on Houston and Crosby in SoHo that overflows with collectible antique bric-a-brac. It reminded me of a store that could have been assembled by Kemal during the decades of unrequited love he endured as he tried to win back Füsun, in Orhan Pamuk's unhappy love story of the same name.

INGREDIENTS

2 oz. dry vermouth

1 oz. absinthe

¼ oz. Jeppson's Malört or three dashes wormwood bitters

INSTRUCTIONS

Pour all ingredients into a mixing glass filled with ice and stir at least 40 times. Strain into a rocks glass.

SUGGESTED VERMOUTHS

Atsby Amberthorn

Ransom Dry

Sutton Cellars Brown Label

Uncouth Wildflower

LAUGHTER AND FORGETTING

ALEX OTT

This cocktail is unlike any you've ever had. You have to try it to believe it, because it doesn't look quite right on paper. It is proof positive that you can't believe everything you read, and that you need to go out and experience something to truly understand it. It's perfect for the end of the night, when you do not want to forget what is about to happen.

*BURNT SUGAR INSTRUCTIONS

To prepare burnt-sugar syrup, simply add 10 tsp. of brown sugar or evaporated cane sugar to 1 cup of boiling water. Bring to a simmer and cook until the water becomes viscous and dark brown. Stop heating when you detect a caramel scent.

*WHIPPED CREAM INSTRUCTIONS

To prepare freshly whipped cream, add 1 tsp. of regular sugar to 2 oz. heavy whipping cream and whip until peaks form and when the cream is on the verge of hardening. It still needs to be liquid enough to flow onto the cocktail surface.

CORDIAL

INGREDIENTS

1½ oz. dry vermouth

1 oz. cranberry juice

½ oz. burnt-sugar syrup*

2 parts of freshly made whipped cream*

1 tsp. sugar

1 small handful of chocolate flakes

INSTRUCTIONS

Combine the vermouth, cranberry juice, and burnt syrup into a shaker filled with ice, shake, and strain into a cordial glass. Carefully place the opening of the whipped cream cocktail tin onto the rim of the glass and slowly let the cream distribute across the surface. When the surface is finally covered, stop pouring. Garnish with chocolate flakes.

COLLINS

INGREDIENTS

2 oz. Atsby Armadillo Cake Vermouth

¾ oz. Hudson Baby Bourbon

2 tbsp. fresh blackberry puree

4 oz. sparkling water

1 blackberry

1 lemon peel

INSTRUCTIONS

Pour the vermouth, bourbon, and blackberry puree into a cocktail shaker and shake vigorously. Strain into a mason jar or Collins glass filled with cubes of ice, and top with sparkling water. Garnish with blackberry and lemon peel.

CUNNING LITTLE VIXEN

This cocktail was first served at the Manhattan Cocktail Classic in 2013. It was so good that it landed the bartender Josh Sontag on the cover of the *Wall Street Journal*'s Dining Section and it was listed as the top cocktail that year by several national publications. Smooth, sweet, and refreshing, it's a perfect cap to a late night.

COUPE

STIFF LITTLE FINGERS

JOSH SONTAG, BRESLIN LOBBY BAR,
ACE HOTEL, NYC

INGREDIENTS

1¾ oz. Atsby Armadillo Cake

1¼ oz. Hudson New York Corn Whiskey

¼ oz. simple syrup

INSTRUCTIONS

Pour ingredients into a mixing glass and stir until very cold. Strain into a coupe.

Shortly after Atsby launched, the company formed a friendship with the high-end sex-toy shop Babeland, and we began teaming up with them to teach workshops on sex toys and vermouth (the aromatics in vermouth, as described earlier, being closely tied to intimacy and eroticism). We needed a good name for a signature cocktail, and the night before the first workshop I was out at a concert listening to the English band The Beat. Some guy walked past wearing a ripped and faded concert-T that said Stiff Little Fingers. It turned out that they were a punk rock band from Belfast, and that they had the perfect name for the following night's class. The secret to this drink is using a very good moonshine. There are a lot of them on the market nowadays (and a lot of bad ones too).

SCENTS OF EDEN

JOSH SONTAG, BRESLIN LOBBY BAR,
ACE HOTEL, NYC

COLLINS   ROCKS   WINE

Cocktails should smell as good as they taste, and the secret to making cocktails that smell good is to use good-smelling ingredients. This is especially true of cocktails that you're drinking later in the night, particularly if you've been drinking previously and your taste buds are no longer as perceptive. Your sense of smell will kick in if the drink is highly aromatic, and it will make the experience just as enjoyable as the first sip of your evening's first drink, despite the dampened taste bud receptors. Using citrus helps, but using a highly aromatic vermouth along with a flavored syrup will round off the drink's aroma.

INGREDIENTS

1½ oz. sweet vermouth

1½ oz. fig reduction (figs and simple syrup in a pot, boiled down 15 minutes)

½ oz. London dry gin

½ oz. lemon juice

1 sliced fig

INSTRUCTIONS

Build ingredients in a cocktail shaker with four ice cubes, and shake vigorously. Strain into a Collins, rocks, or wine glass. Top with soda water and garnish with a fig slice.

SUGGESTED VERMOUTHS

Atsby Armadillo Cake

Hammer & Tongs Sac'Résine or L'Afrique

ACKNOWLEDGMENTS

Obviously, this book is not possible without the incredible selfless help from the people I am fortunate enough to call my community and family. They deserve more than just words, but for now, let me give at least that, in no particular order: my agent Jess Regel, who knows how to spot a diamond in the rough; Reka Nyari for her beautiful photographs; Alex Ott for styling the cocktails like nobody's business; Mark and Melissa Bamber for the use of their beautiful home and cocktail glasses; Melissa Bamber Home for pillows and wallpaper as backdrops; Sother Teague, Franky Marshal, Pam Witznizer, Michael Neff, for their cocktail creations; Garry Severin for talking to me about vermouth in cocktails just because I asked; Josh Sontag for his many amazing cocktails and professional review and editing of all the cocktails; Amy Zavatto for her thoughtful reads and comments on my manuscripts; Dan Marotta, my lawyer (enough said); Amor Y Amargo, Ace Hotel, Astor Wine & Spirits, and Madame X for the gracious use of their spaces for the photographs; Bianca Miraglia for creating such delicious vermouths and important edits and commentary; Carl Sutton, Andrew Quady, Patrick Taylor, Tad Steestedt for their delicious vermouths and willingness to share insights and secrets; Zack Manna, Suzanne Salvatore, Matthew Ford for his invaluable historical research; Jordan Zimmerman for her research and teaching me how to pair cheese and vermouth; Paul Clarke for screaming from the roof-tops about vermouth for years; Russell Hearn and the entire crew at Premium Wine Group for being so awesome, Hanna Lee Communications; and Heath Jones for asking me "What are you afraid of?" before I started this project.

Special thanks to my editors at The Countryman Press, the amazing Ann Treistman and Dan Crissman, who made this book what it is. Then there is Kimberly Coombs, who designed the perfect cover (and all things Atsby). I'd also like to thank my parents, Ron and Harriet Ford, for my roots and wings (and teaching me to love the craft of writing and taking chances); Joseph and Joanna Jiampietro for their tremendous support; my two children, Anker and Tessa who teach me something new everyday; and my wife, Glynis, for so many things it would fill a book, so I'll just say for everything.

ENDNOTES

1   Patrick E. McGovern, *Uncorking the Past* (Berkeley: University of California Press, 2009), 65.

2   Gas chromatography–mass spectrometry (GC-MS); high-performance liquid chromatography–mass spectrometry (HPLC-MS); Fourier-transform infrared spectrometry (FT-IR); stable isotope analysis; and selective Feigl spot tests.

3   Patrick E. McGovern et al., "Fermented Beverages of Pre- and Proto-Historic China," *Proceedings of the National Academy of Sciences* 101, no. 51 (December 21, 2004): 17597.

4   McGovern, *Uncorking the Past*, 47.

5   Ibid., 54.

6   Patrick E. McGovern, Stuart Fleming, and Solomon Katz, *The Origins and Ancient History of Wine*, Food and Nutrition in History and Anthropology, Book 11 (Luxembourg: Gordon and Breach, 1995).

7   Pedanius Dioscorides, *De Materia Medica* I.25.

8   Of the remaining seven plants, all are arguably native to the southern Levant.

9   Kazim Abdullaev, "Sacred Plants and the Cultic Beverage Haoma," Comparative Studies of South Asia, Africa and the Middle East, Vol. 30 No. 3, 2010, 335.

10   Ibid.

11   Xinru Liu, *The Silk Road in World History* (New York: Oxford University Press, 2010), 36.

12   Ibid., 38.

13   Dalby, *Dangerous Tastes*, 91.

14   *Dangerous Tastes*, 37.

15   Ibid. citing Pliny, *Natural History* 12, 87-8.

16   Dalby, *Dangerous Tastes*, 129.

17   Cyrus Redding, *A History and Description of Modern Wines* (London: Whittaker, Treacher, & Arnot, 1833), 7.

18   William Eamon, *The Professor of Secrets: Mystery, Medicine, and Alchemy in Renaissance Italy* (Washington, D.C.: National Geographic Society, 2010), 37.

19   Dioscorides, *Materia Medica* 2.82.5.

20   Dioscorides, *Materia Medica* 2.82.5.

21   Aegineta Paulus, *The Seven Books of Paulus Aegineta*, 64.

22   *The Natural History of Pliny*, Volume 3, Chapter 19.

23   *Dangerous Tastes*, 134–35.

24   William Eamon, *The Professor of Secrets: Mystery, Medicine, and Alchemy in Renaissance Italy*, pg. 75

25   Dalby, *Dangerous Tastes*, 129, citing Dioscorides, *Materia Medica*, 5.39.

26   G. Ruscelli, *The Secrets of the Reverend Maister Alexis*, f.36r.

27   Ibid.

28   Ibid.

29   Paul Freedman, *Out of the East: Spices and the Medieval Imagination* (New Haven: Yale University Press, 2008). Piment recipe edited from a record in the cathedral archives of Girona, Catalonia, and published in Pep Vila, "El Piment, una beguda confegida a la catedral de Girona durant el segle XIV," *Annals de l'Institut d'Estudis Gironins* 40 (1999). The first recipe for Piment appears in 1182 by Chrétien de Troyes.

30   André Louis Simon, *The History of the Wine Trade in England* (London: Wyman & Sons, 1907). pg. 250.

31   Ibid.

32   Theophrastus, *On Odours*, 7.32.

33   Dioscorides, *Materia Medica*, I.64.

34   Ibid.

35   Dalby, *Dangerous Tastes*, 129, citing *Geoponica* 8.25.

36   Ibid., 130, citing *Apicius* I.I.

37   Donna R. Barnes & Peter G. Rose, *Matters of Taste: Food and Drink in Seventeenth-Century Dutch Art and Life* (Syracuse: Syracuse University Press, 2002).

38   Kirstin Kennedy, "Sharing and Status: The Design and Function of a Sixteenth-Century Spanish Spice Stand in the Victoria and Albert Museum," in Peta Motture & Michelle O'Malley (eds.), *Re-thinking Renaissance Objects: Design, Function and Meaning* (The Society for Renaissance Studies and Blackwell Publishing Ltd., 2011).

39   The first recipe for Hippocras in English appears in the 1390 publication, *Forme of Cury.* For the next two hundred years dozens of books reprinted substantially similar recipes. The website oldcook.com compiled a bibliography of books where such recipes are found: in1393, *Ménagier de Paris;* 15th century, the printed edition of the *Viandier de Taillevent;* 1508, *The booke of Kervinge and Sewing;* 1529, *Libro de guisados*, Ruperto de Nola (version in castillan of *Llibre del Coch*); 1555, *La pratique de faire toutes confitures, condiments, distillations d'eaux odoriférantes & plusieurs autres recettes très utiles* (6 recipes of hippocras and one receipe of Piment); 1593, *Secreti*, Stefano Francesco di Romolo Rossetti; 1600, *Le théâtre d'agriculture et mesnage des champs,* Olivier de Serres, 1607, *Le trésor de santé,* 1660, *Le confiturier françois,* Massialot; 1689, *Le sieur de La Varanne,* recipe of white hippocras; 1692, *La Maison réglée d'Audiger:* to make a good white and red hippocras, 1723; *The cooks and confectioners Dictionary,* John Nott; 18th century, *Le Petit Albert:* to make rapidly an excellent hippocras; 1768, *Le Cannameliste français;* 1850, *La cuisinière de la campagne et de la ville* (The country and city cook).

40   Lawrence Norfolk, *John Saturnall's Feast* (from the *Book of John Saturnall,* 1681). Also, in the 1736 ninth edition of *Pharmacopœia officinalis & extemporanea,* or *A complete English dispensatory,* by John Quincy,. Quincy's recipe calls, on page 554, for an ounce each of cloves and ginger, 2 ounces of nutmeg and cinnamon, along with 12 pounds of sweet wine and 3½ pounds of fine sugar, as well as new milk, one lemon, and a few sprigs of rosemary.

41   André Louis Simon, *The History of the Wine Trade in England* (London: Wyman & Sons, 1907). pg. 252.

42   "Ressaite to make Ypocras," according to Arnold's *Chronicle,* was as follows:"For a gallon and pynt of red wyn, take synamon iii unic, ginger, dryed an unce, greynes and longe poper di unce, cloues and masys, a q'rt of an unce, spignard a quatir of an unce, sugar ii lb."

43   Ken Albala, *The Banquet: Dining in the great courts of Late Renaissance Europe* (Champaign: University of Illinois Press, 2007), 111–12.

44   Tracy Thong, "Performance of the Banquet Course in Early Modern Drama," in Joan Fitzpatrick (ed.), Renaissance Food from Rabelais to Shakespeare: Culinary Readings and Culinary Histories (Burlington, VT: Ashgate Publishing Company, 2010), 107–8.

45   Gustave Flaubert, Madame Bovary, trans. Margaret Mauldon (Oxford: Oxford University Press, 2004), 266.

46   While the author of *Il Vermouth di Torino* states that this is the first time such a recipe has been published in Italian, identical recipes were published two hundred years previously in the Don Alessio's *Secrets.*

47   Blagojević Pl, Radulović N, Palić R, Stojanović G., Chemical composition of the essential oils of serbian wild-growing *Artemisia absinthium* and Artemisia vulgaris, J Agric Food Chem. 2006 Jun 28;54(13):4780-9.

48   Temple Henry Croker, *Complete dictionary of arts and sciences* (London: J. Wilson & J. Fell, 1766).

49   Carpano publication from 1960s.

50   *Vini Itali.* 1:61 63-64.

51   *LIFE* magazine, October 20, 1941, 116.

52   Henry Collins Brown, Valentine's Manual of Old New York, 1923, pg 134.

53   McGovern, *Uncorking the Past,* 333.

54   As a result, Native North Americans gravitated toward mushrooms and tobacco in place of alcohol. See ibid., 337.

55   This belief remained until 1935, more than fifty years after the Continental Army Surgeon General Dr. Benjamin Rush published "An Inquiry into the effects of Ardent Spirits," which ended with a recommendation that the Army stop distributing rum to its soldiers. Noah Rothbaum, *The Business of Spirits* (Kaplan Publishing: Routledge, 2007).

56   David Wondrich, *Imbibe!* (New York: Perigree, 2007), 154

57   By David Wondrich, *Imbibe!,* pg, 234.

58   Charles Dickens, *Dictionary of Paris,* 1883.

59   There were no French producers at this exhibit, although Noilly Prat shipped its first shipment of dry vermouth to San Francisco this year. It had shipped some dry vermouth to New Orleans two years prior. See Wondrich, *Imbibe!,* 112. Surviving paperwork suggests that Noilly Pratt shipped its first bottles to New York in 1844.

60   Edwin G. Burrows and Mike Wallace, *Gotham: A History of New York City to 1898* (New York: Oxford University Press, 2000), 697.

61   Ibid., 700.

62   "When New York Was Really Wicked: I-Satan's Circus," *The New Yorker,* December 3, 1927, 25.

63   Ibid.

64   Howard Zinn, *A People's History of the United States* (New York: Harper & Row, 1980), 330.

65   William Bobo, *Glimpses of New York City* (1852).

66   Burrows & Wallace, *Gotham,* 726.

67   Ibid, 804.

68   Ibid, 996.

69   Zinn, *A People's History,* at pg. 433.

70   William Lawrence Slout, *Broadway Below the Sidewalk: Concert Saloons of old New York,* Clipper Studies in the Theatre 4, (Wildside Press, 1994), 27.

71   Wondrich, *Imbibe!,* 208.

72   William F. Mulhall, Valentine's Manual of New York, 1923, pg 134

73   Dickens, *Dictionary of Paris,* 1883, pg. 49.

74   Sol Steinmet, *There's a Word for It: The Explosion of the American Language Since 1900.*

75   New York Times, New Corporations, November 17, 1894.

76   "Annual Report on Commission of Patents, 1914." Cinzano (Italian), Noilly Prat (France) and Chaurain & Cie (France) also all had patents by this date.

77   "Contraband Liquors Seized," *New York Times,* July 17, 1884.

78   Harry Johnson, *New and Improved Bartenders Manual,* 1900, 151.

79   "To Increase the Revenue: Hearings Before the Subcommittee of the Committee on Finance, United States Senate, Sixty-fourth

Congress, First Session, on H.R. 16763, an Act to Increase the Revenue, and for Other Purposes," July 17–August 1, 1916.

80 Italian regulations also addressed requirements for "Vermut amaro," "vermut dry," vermut toscano," vermut di Sicilia," "Vermut chinato," vermut al Bitter," vermut alia vainiglia," "vermut al Barolo," and Vermut al Marsala."

81 *Consular Reports: Commerce, Manufactures, Etc.* Volume 60.

82 *Journal of the Society of Arts*, August 11, 1897.

83 Ettore Molinari, "Treatise on General and Industrial Organic Chemistry," vol. 1 (1921).

84 Doris Lanier, *Absinthe—the Cocaine of the Nineteenth Century* (McFarland, 2004), 3–5.

85 Robert Townsend, *Travels in Hungary: With a Short Account of Vienna in the Year 1793*. A Viennese traveler named Selden Edwards traversed lower Hungry in 1818 and encountered small quantities of Ausbruch, and some of those preparations of wine were called "wermuth." Edwards noted there were two sorts of wermuth, Palunita and Tropwermuth. The exact process of forming the latter was a secret, but the former is prepared by putting together fresh grapes, wormwood, bruised mustard-seed, and several spices into layers in a cask, pouring old wine over the whole, and closing the cask firmly. In a few weeks, the liquor is fit for use, but it will keep above a year, and "though much esteemed, it seldom forms an article of commerce." The same traveler came upon a large vineyard belonging to Prince Esterházy. It was at this vineyard that he witnessed the making of a "famous aromatic cordial, made by boiling wormwood and some other herbs in new wine." What is so noteworthy about this experience, if it is even true, is that it has been reported that the small vineyard had belonged to the Esterházy family for generations, and although it was rumored to have produced the best wines in all of Europe, "no one has tasted them save the Esterházys and half of Franz Joseph's fabled aristocracy and their fortunate guests." In *A History and Description of Modern Wines*, Cyrus Redding notes that "the wines called Palunia and tropfwermuth pass under the general name of Wermuth. They are a preparation of grapes with wormwood, seeds, and spices of different kinds over which they pour old wine, and cork it up. It is drunk at home and rarely exported. This, too, is a wine used medicinally, and drunk as a mixed wine." See also, *The Lost Prince: A Novel* by Selden Edwards.

86 Charles Dickens, *Dictionary of Paris* (1883).

87 Kingsley Amis, Everyday Drinking: The Distilled Kingsley Amis, pg. 45.

88 Paul Clarke, Imbibe Magazine, American Beauty: Domestic winemakers are doing vermouth their own way, September/October 2012.

89 Ibid, 2.

90 "Notices of Judgment under the Food and Drug Act," Issue 5101, Part 6000, September 6, 1917.

91 Richard Poulin, *Graphic Design + Architecture, A 20th-Century History* (Beverly, MA: Rockport Publishers, 2012), 61.

92 Nannette Stone, *The Little Black Book of Martinis* (White Plains, NY: Peter Pauper Press, 2004).

93 *The New Yorker*, May 12, 1934, News from the Wine Country, pg. 66.

94 Ibid.

95 *House and Garden*, vol. 65, Conde Naste, 1934.

96 http://thewayweate.net/post/20043311267/cora-vermouth-advertisement-gourmet-march-1960.

97 Ibid.

98 William Grimes, *Straight Up or On the Rocks: The Story of the American Cocktail* (New York: North Point Press, 2001).

99 B. B. Turner, "The Importance of Vermouth," *Wines and Vines* 22:3, 1941.

100 Ibid.

101 Otto F. Jacoby, "Developing the Vermouth Formula," *Wines & Vines*, April 1948.

102 Ibid.

103 H. Otto Sichel, "Vermouth: Its Production and Future," *Wines & Vines* 1945.

104 *The New Yorker*, October 6, 1945, pg. 86.

105 *The New Yorker*, November 10, 1945, pg. 107.

106 Thomas Pinney, *A History of Wine in America: From Prohibition to the Present* (Berkeley: UC Press, 2005), pg. 225.

107 U.S. Bureau of Alcohol, Tobacco, and Firearms, 1971.

108 David A. Embury, *The Fine Art of Mixing Drinks*, 2nd ed. (New York: Garden City Books: 1952).

109 Bernard DeVoto, *The Hour: A Cocktail Manifesto* (Cambridge, MA: Riverside Press, 1948), 56

110 E. B. White, "Notes and Comment," *The New Yorker*, December 4, 1948, 25.

111 *LIFE*, July 25, 1955.

112 Atomizer or not, vermouth consumption in the United States still couldn't be slowed. Consumption was up to 2,519,765 cases by 1958, a 4.6 percent increase over the prior year.

113 *LIFE*, February 24, 1958.

114 *LIFE*, November 24, 1967.

115 *LIFE*, December 10, 1946.

116 M&R advertisement, April 6, 1940.

117 Iain Topliss, *The Comic Worlds of Peter Arno, William Steig, Charles Addams and Saul Steinberg* (Baltimore: The Johns Hopkins University Press, 2005).

118 *The New Yorker*, November 15, 1958.

119 *The New Yorker*, November 15, 1958.

120 *The New Yorker*, June 9, 1941.

121 *The New Yorker*, November 3, 1956.

122 Advertisement, March 10, 1934.

123 *The New Yorker*, March 12,, 1960, pg. 159

124 Peter Valaer, *Wines of the World* (New York: Abelard Press, 1950).

125 Lejon advertisement, August 13, 1960.

126 Cresta advertisement, November 6, 1954

127 Under United States law, all vermouth must be at least 75 percent grape wine. The list of permissible ingredients can found in the Code of Federal Regulations.

128 Thomas Pinney, *A History of Wine in America: From Prohibition to the Present*, pg. 202

129 Raymond J. Folwell and John L. Baritelle, *The U.S. Wine Market* (Washington, D.C.: U.S. Department of Agriculture, Economics, Statistics, and Cooperatives Service, Agricultural Economic Report No. 417., 1978).

130 Patrick E. McGovern, whose work I've already cited several times, is the leading authority on ancient alcoholic beverages. His book, *Uncorking the Past: The Quest for Wine, Beer, and Other Alcoholic Beverages,* is a whirlwind tour around the ancient world that conclusively establishes him as the world's foremost expert on this topic.

131 Sutton bottles about half of the total volume of each batch and leaves the remaining product as "mother batch" for the next production.

132 Daniel J. Levitin, *This Is Your Brain on Music* (New York: Plume/Penguin, 2007), 140–144.

133 Kingsley Amis, *Everyday Drinking: The Distilled Kingsley Amis* (New York: Bloomsbury, 2010), 132.

134 Bruce Watson, "We've Seen The Future With Small Batch American Vermouth," *Food Republic*, February 11, 2013.

135 Jack Bettridge, "A New Approach to Vermouth," *Wine Spectator*, October 15, 2013.

136 Alice Feiring, "American Vermouth: Anything Goes," *The New York Times*, February 12, 2013.

137 Kara Newman, "Eight New Vermouths," *Wine Enthusiast Magazine*, Web 2012, http://www.winemag.com/Web-2012/Nine-New-Vermouths.

138 "American Vermouth: As Told by Atsby Founder Adam Ford," *Drinking in America*, June 30, 2013, http://www.drinkinginamerica.com/american-vermouth-as-told-by-atsby-founder-adam-ford.

139 Erica Ducey, Vermouth on the Rise, Saveur Magazine, October 7, 2014.

140 "Vermouth Seminar at Manhattan Cocktail Classic," *Storied Sips*, http://storiedsips.com/ailec_event/vermouth-seminar-at-manhattan-cocktail-classic/?instance_id.

141 Paul Richardson, "Barcelona's New Vermouth Bars," *Financial Times*, August 16, 2013.

142 Martin Doudoroff, "Vermouth by Brand," Vermouth 101, http://vermouth101.com/vermouths.html.

143 "Murray's Classes," *Murray's Cheese*, http://www.murrayscheese.com/classes.html.

144 William Schmidt, *The Flowing Bowl: When and What to Drink* (New York: Charles L. Webster & Co., 1891), xv.

145 Calvin Trillin, *The New Yorker*, June 7, 1982.

146 The People Newspaper (now the Sunday People), 1925

INDEX

Sunday Morning, 180–81
Sutton, Carl, 145–47
Sutton Cellars Brown Label Vermouth, 145–47
Sutton & Soda, 147
syrups
    burnt-sugar, 219
    fig reduction, 225
    ginger, 176
    simple, 222
    tobacco, 207

T
Tea Time, 192–93

U
Uncouth Vermouth, 160–61

V
vermouth
    American vs. European, 154–56, 173
    filtration process for, 148
    name origin of, 23, 98
    regulation of, 92–93, 115, 151–53, 167
    wormwood use in, 21, 96–99
vermouth, history of. *See* American culture, vermouth in; American vermouth, twenty-first century; history of vermouth; wermut (vermouth), history of
The Vermouth Cocktail
    history of, 66–67
    recipe for, 68–69

vermouth cocktails
    aperitif cocktails, 189–199
    brunch cocktails, 175–87
    late-night cocktails, 213–25
    modern cocktails, 201–11
    recipe construction of, 172–73
    See also The Vermouth Cocktail
Vermouth Martini, 161
Vermouth & Soda, 185
vodka
    Cornelia, 176–77
    El Papi, 153
    Pale End of Day, 196–97
Vya Vermouth, 141–44

W
wermut (vermouth), history of, 56–57, 61–64
    See also The Vermouth Cocktail
whiskey
    Stiff Little Fingers, 222–23
    Sunday Morning, 180–81
    See also rye
White Negroni, 190–91
    See also Negroni
wine. *See* aromatized wines; medicinal wines
wine, botrytized, 163
wormwood (Artemisia absinthium)
    medicinal claims, 40, 62, 96–97
    medicinal properties of, 58–59
    as vermouth ingredient, 21, 96–99, 115
    wine from, 40, 43, 47, 61–62

CREDITS

Page 14: © zulufriend/iStockPhoto.com; pages 22, 140, 156: Glynis Gotwald Ford; page 27: © itsme23/iStockPhoto.com; page 41: Rogers Fund, 1913; page 67: B. W. Kilburn, Library of Congress; page 79: Theodore Sedgwick, Library of Congress; page 81: Nagel & Weingartner, Library of Congress; page 102: New York World-Telegram and the Sun Newspaper Photograph Collection, Library of Congress; page 138: © maurese/iStockPhoto.com; page 152: Neil Kopplin, Imbue Cellars